SCHMEICHEL
The Autobiography

SCHMEICHEL
The Autobiography

Peter Schmeichel
with Egon Balsby

Virgin

First published in Great Britain in 1999 by
Virgin Books
an imprint of Virgin Publishing
Thames Wharf Studios
Rainville Road
London W6 9HA

A catalogue record for this book is available
from the British Library.

ISBN 1 85227 867 6

Typeset by TW Typesetting, Plymouth, Devon
Printed in Great Britain by Creative Print and
Design (Wales), Ebbw Vale

Contents

'The buy of the century'

'I don't believe a better goalkeeper played the game. He is a giant figure in the history of United.'

Sir Alex Ferguson on Peter Schmeichel

Acknowledgements

The publishers would like to thank the following for permission to reproduce photographs: Allsport, Empics, Colorsport, Action Images, Action-Plus, EPA/Nordfoto and Peter Schmeichel.

Translation from Danish into English by Carl King and Hugh Matthews.

Career record section collated by Ivan Ponting.

Thanks to Anne Mette Palm of publishers Borsen in Copenhagen, and to Ole Frederiksen.

1 The Last Dance

'Sir Alex confessed that he hadn't been able to see any way in which we could get back into the game; in other words, he had all but conceded defeat when he saw his goalkeeper rushing up the pitch like a madman. He had simply lost his overall view of the game. He was not able to see that there was a real point at that stage of the game in putting the German defence under intense pressure.'

M Y VERY LAST GAME for Manchester United is about to kick off. There are over 90,000 spectators inside Catalonia's cathedral of football, the Nou Camp. They produce an incredible noise. It's a fantastic atmosphere for both finalists in the 1999 European Cup.

It's 26 May, and for us it's the last of eleven days during which we have had the chance to secure three of the most coveted prizes in international club football. We have already won the English Premier League. The FA Cup final against Newcastle was a walkover, a convincing 2–0 victory. Now we have come out on to Barcelona's famous and enormous grass carpet in our quest to hammer home the last nail and get our hands on the prestigious European Cup, last seen in the club's trophy cabinet in 1968.

It is just over six months since I announced at a press conference in Manchester that this would be my last season with United after eight contented and successful years, almost a whole lifetime in football with the most fantastic club in the world. In 90 minutes' time it would all be over, and either we or Bayern Munich – also in pursuit of a domestic treble – would be able to raise the great cup towards the sky and receive the traditional roar of approval.

The game was being transmitted live to two billion people, but for United's supporters and the players on the pitch it possessed that extra dimension: a victory for us would mean that we had achieved the almost unattainable, the fabled Treble, and bring the long-lost trophy back to Manchester again. I was so focused on this that I honestly didn't give a thought to the fact that it was my very last appearance for the team. It was a football match just like all the others, and it had to be won. There was no room for sentimental reflection within the ring of concentration I have always built up around myself in the lead-up to a match.

Before the game, Alex Ferguson had given us one of his more beguiling and emotional team talks: 'There isn't a team in the world who play as well as you do. And that's why you mustn't be afraid. There's no reason to be. No team can beat you if you play at the level you are capable of – and of course that's what you'll do. I am very proud, and honoured, about what you've already given for me and the club. The only thing I regret is that I can't send you all out on to the pitch. As you know, we're only allowed to play with eleven men, but all of you without exception deserve to be out there today.' Of course, he didn't mention our obvious handicap on the night: both Roy Keane and Paul Scholes were suspended. With his usual confidence, Ferguson took it for granted that David Beckham and Nicky Butt would be more than capable of holding their own in midfield.

But from the moment the bald-headed and highly competent Italian referee Pierluigi Collina blew his whistle for the start of the game, Bayern Munich came at us hard, and five minutes later the ball lay in the back of the net behind me. The Germans had been awarded a free kick a good distance outside the penalty area on the left. I directed my wall, as always, but at the very moment Mario Basler moved towards the ball, Carsten Jancker threw himself straight into our cover and displaced the man in the middle. At that very same second, Basler sent the ball thundering towards the goal at an angle I simply hadn't anticipated. It should never have been allowed to happen, but we had to swallow it: the Germans had a precious 1–0 lead.

But immediately we began to dominate as the Germans – automatically, and, as it proved later, quite disastrously – assumed a highly vigilant defensive formation which, admittedly, worked extremely well in the first half.

I knew that Ferguson's half-time analysis was going to be

interesting. He grabbed hold of me and let me know that we had played a bloody awful game from the start, and he wanted to know what the hell had happened, giving away a goal like that! I wasn't in the mood for an argument, so Ferguson changed his strategy as quick as a flash, and said to the throng: 'But in the last twenty minutes you played fantastic! Do you realise how many times you could have scored?' The fact was that we hadn't really been anywhere near the German goal. But he planted a seed of hope in us, and it certainly seemed as if we had been transformed when we went out for the second half.

Just before we left the changing room, Ferguson had added: 'Lads, when you go out there, just have a look at that cup! It will be about five yards away from you, but you won't be able to touch it, of course. And I want you to think about the fact that if you lose this game you'll have been so close to it. And you will hate that thought for the rest of your lives. So just make sure you don't f*****g lose!' A very shrewd point. In one way it was almost recklessly bold, but at the same time it emphasised that he had not for one moment forgotten our aim or the immense importance of this game for Manchester United.

Everyone who saw that game knows that it didn't really come to a head until the very end. Before that happened, Ferguson, with his customary precision and intuition, had brought on Teddy Sheringham to replace Jesper Blomqvist, and a little while later he took off Andy Cole and threw on our Norwegian bomber, Ole Gunnar Solskjaer – two moves which in the space of two minutes or so made a world of difference, wiping the smiles from the Germans' faces. Once again, we had demonstrated that a football match isn't over until the fat lady sings.

First, in about the 89th minute, we won a corner. From my position in goal it was clear that something pretty extraordinary had to happen. That's why I raced up the pitch right into Bayern Munich's penalty area. I knew I would make a nuisance of myself, and my green goalkeeper's jersey managed to cause considerable confusion. I had three men around me and, in the kind of chaos defenders dread,

Sheringham, as he has done so often before, managed to get his foot to the ball. It rocketed into the net to the left of Oliver Kahn, giving him no chance at all. I have no doubt whatsoever that my sudden rush up the pitch was a contributory factor in that goal. And I have to admit that, without worrying about it in the slightest, I ignored Alex Ferguson's vigorous body language which signalled unmistakably that I should get back to my goal immediately. We laughed quite a bit about it afterwards.

That goal seemed to shatter the Germans, perhaps understandably, and certainly gave us that extra motivation to draw on our very last resources. About a minute later it led to yet another vital effort from Sheringham. From a corner kick on the left, he headed the ball down into the area where Solskjaer, with unfailing certainty, drove it into the roof of the net. He made the shot look so easy, but actually that kind of timing and direction demands the finest touch of technique – not to mention composure.

It was the killer blow. After 31 years, and many years of striving throughout the 1990s, Manchester United had returned to the throne of European club football. I felt an intense mixture of immense personal pride and joyful humility, and I was delighted that I was able to play a part in re-establishing Manchester United where they belong: at the very top.

It may be true that the final was not a particularly spectacular football match. Finals seldom are, because everything has to be decided on the night. This often leads to a tight, tactical confrontation, but the final minutes of this game are surely destined to be written up at some length in football's history books.

And in the face of the thoughts of others – the Germans and a number of expert football journalists, for example – that Bayern Munich deserved to win, I will always stand up to disagree. Why? You can easily make out a case that during the 1998/99 season Manchester United played the most entertaining football that has ever been seen in the Champions' League. I certainly don't remember ever having seen another team that played such attacking football and took so many chances in order to capture the title. Our motto throughout the campaign was 'Forward, forward!' – without, of course, leaving ourselves open at the back – and it was naturally based on the collective confidence that had developed over the last six months or so, during which time we had played 34 consecutive games without defeat, and in doing so had collected all the trophies we could on our way. This conviction was allied to the underlying philosophy of our team, which was the simplest of all: We just need to score one goal more than the opposition, irrespective of how the balance of possession, or any other irrelevant statistic, reads after the 90 minutes. In this manner we managed to do what no team before us had done.

But in the end it was naturally all down to Alex Ferguson. He had built up the team, put his trust unfailingly in its ability to deliver, arranged the necessary transfers and blended the new players in with the existing squad, which included many products of United's own youth scheme.

And it has been a gradual process. The road that led to the fantastic display of football we were able to put on in the 1998/99 season was not an easy one – blood, sweat and tears have been shed on the way. The previous season we were also in the Champions' League, but the team was still not sufficiently polished. We simply lacked the killer instinct. We were not cool enough, and our play was inevitably restricted by an unavoidable tactical straitjacket. That was essential for a team under construction, like scaffolding around a fledgling building, but the bonus was that the tactical elements were gradually transformed into automatic reflexes.

We eventually reached the point where players knew their roles in their sleep. No one was in doubt about whether they needed to run backward or forward. They positioned themselves intuitively according to the way in which play was developing, and they made themselves available for overlaps at lightning speed. The Manchester United team of 1999 played so well together, with so much control of the ball and such inbuilt determination, that the result was a host of scoring chances, many of them converted, not least in the final stages of a game when an opponent had been worn down.

We played well in many of the games on the way to the final, and I was bursting with pride as Manchester United prepared to receive the European Cup on that magical night in the Nou Camp. As captain – I had taken over the armband when Roy Keane's suspension prevented him from taking part in the final – I was led to believe that first of all I would receive the cup. But there was a slight mix-up in UEFA's organisation of the presentation ceremony and a new procedure had been decided upon without anybody informing us: the championship medals were to be presented first, and after that the cup itself.

So, blissfully ignorant of this, I walked forward, full of anticipation, to accept the big-eared trophy on behalf of my team. I was presented with my medal and then I stood there waiting, so long in fact that it started to get a bit embarrassing. Eventually I slunk off as nonchalantly as I could, but I was rather irritated by the fact that I had to line up behind the squad again. Once more I filed forward towards the silver cup, which in terms of personal triumphs can be placed alongside the European Championship trophy Denmark had captured seven years previously after that fantastic final in the gloaming at Gothenburg.

At last, it was my turn again. And suddenly, there I was holding it. I gave it a huge smack of a kiss. You don't really feel normal on an evening like that. Our fantastic, faithful fans followed my every movement with bated breath, and when I held up the cup towards the black sky of Barcelona and the roar broke loose, I genuinely felt as if I was at Old Trafford.

It's difficult to explain the feeling that rushes through your body when you lift up the most important trophy in Europe in the direction of 45,000 ecstatic fans. In a way, you can compare it with being handed your newborn child in the delivery room. And then you have to multiply that roughly by a factor of two. There aren't many things that surpass the sensation of seeing your child for the first time, but that is the sort of experience most people have the opportunity to savour at least once in a lifetime. There are not many people who get the chance to hold aloft the European Cup to a roar of excitement. That is what makes it a little bit more special.

Back in the changing room after the game, I naturally had discussions with both Alex Ferguson and our assistant coach, Steve McClaren, about my sprint into the Bayern Munich penalty area at the end of the game. I have to admit that I was a little bit disappointed with Ferguson, because he had always given me the impression that he would consider it a lack of winning instinct if I didn't go up at the end of a game which was slipping away from us and attempt to decide it in our favour. He confessed that he just hadn't been able to see any way in which we could get back into the game; in other words, he had all but conceded defeat when he saw his goalkeeper rushing up the pitch like a madman. He had simply lost his overall view of the game. He was not able to see that there was a real point at that stage of the game in putting the German defence under intense pressure.

As far as Steve was concerned, I think it was simply the fact that at the clubs he had been with before, they had never considered taking chances of this kind, and he was not completely satisfied with what I had done. But he had only been with the club for four months and had perhaps not really got into his soul what it would mean to Manchester United to lose a game like this. Of course, we had a little chat about this after the game on a very friendly basis. I hope that I made Steve realise that it's worth taking chances if you're good enough and the stakes are sky-high.

But it's not only managers and coaches who have reacted strongly towards my apparently rash behaviour as a goalkeeper. Many other people have asked me since the game: 'How the hell did you have the nerve to run upfield? There were two billion people watching you, and you'd have made a complete fool of yourself if the Germans had managed to score in an open goal!' I have only one thing to say to this: the possibility didn't cross my mind. If they had scored immediately afterwards, it wouldn't have worried me at all. A 2–0 defeat is no worse than a 1–0 defeat in a final. And this was a major final – it had to be won. When you're losing, there is only one way to go, and that is straight towards your opponent's goal. Manchester United's duty was to score, to get a draw, and perhaps even a win. And that is what you have to try to do, at all costs!

It truly was a marvellous evening in Barcelona: a historic achievement for Manchester United, and for myself a completely unforgettable conclusion to eight wonderful years.

2 Farewell at the Top

'I had more or less lost my sense of time and was under the impression that there were at least seven or eight minutes of the game left, so as Dennis Bergkamp placed the ball on the spot the full implications of the penalty kick hadn't really hit me. Looking back on it now, I can see that at that point I was facing one of the most important moments of my career with United. If Bergkamp had scored, we would have been knocked out of the cup. And if that had been the case, I don't think we could have gone on to win the Premiership.'

T HE QUESTION I WAS ASKED most during 1999 was: 'How
can you leave a club with the strongest team in the
world at a time when you're right on top?' And there's
no easy answer to it.

In the first place, in the summer of 1998 during the World
Cup finals in France, when my plans first began to take
shape, I was not in a position to know that Manchester United
would win everything lock, stock and barrel, and by doing so
achieve the status not just of the world's strongest club team,
but of the greatest United team of all time. Of course I had
feeling that the team had reached a formidable standard – had
come of age, so to speak. But there was always the niggling
question of whether or not things would go our way. Every
successful team needs a bit of fortune along the way, and it
doesn't take much bad luck to make a dream of glory
suddenly subside.

But such considerations weren't constantly on my mind
during the World Cup in France. Apart from the footballing
side of the trip, the experience was something of a revelation
for me. The climate, which encouraged outdoor life, was
something that I, after eight years in Manchester, was
certainly not used to. Throughout the championships, I was
only in my hotel room when I had to sleep. The rest of the
time I was outdoors – preferably on the golf course, where I
enjoyed the combination of beautiful natural surroundings,
the murmur of the Mediterranean, the fragrant air and the
warmth. And I said to myself, quite calmly, that this was

where I would like to live – still with football as my mainstay, of course, but preferably played in a slightly lower gear in a less demanding atmosphere, and with more scope for a different life for Bente, the children and myself.

I wouldn't claim that I had fully made up my mind by the time I left France, but at the beginning of August 1998, when the season was about to start, things had fallen into place for my family and myself. There was no question of rushing into things. For me it was essential to take leave of Manchester United in the right way. I have never been the type to slam the door behind me. For me it has always been important to meet my obligations to the full, to fulfil both the expectations I have of myself and those which others have of me. In short, even though I had decided to leave United, there was still a full season in front of me – and, as always, it was the most important season of all.

But I had to let it be known, so I thought about what would be the best way to handle the matter. In the end, I decided to go to the top, to the club's chairman and undisputed boss Martin Edwards. He was the one who had given me the job in the first place, he paid my wages, he was the one I had wrestled with when my contract came up for renewal, and even though he drove a hard bargain he was also a man I trusted. And he deserved to be the first one to hear about my decision.

Edwards reacted precisely as I had expected him to. He was friendly and understanding, and showed the kind of calm reflection which is a necessary part of being the boss of one of the world's greatest football clubs. He then asked me, very politely, if he could be allowed to consider the matter for twenty-four hours before giving me his decision. I was perfectly happy with this, and things turned out as I had expected them to. The next day in his office, Martin Edwards informed me that the club fully accepted my resignation, understood the reasons for it and would not obstruct me in any way. He also emphasised that the club would not make any financial demands on me, partly because of what I had done for the club and partly because they had only paid peanuts – £550,000 – when they bought me from Brondby.

So that was that. I was able to leave the club, free of transfer demands and therefore the captain of my own destiny. But there was still one season left. And there was also a meeting that had to be faced, with my manager and mentor. It wasn't as if I actually dreaded the thought of it, but it has to be understood that Alex Ferguson's blood is at least as red as a Manchester United shirt. The club is his life, the team is his life, and other people deciding to cut off one of its limbs is a very serious matter.

But all my fears were unfounded. He was just as understanding as Martin Edwards, although the conversation developed in a rather different way. Everything had been agreed after the first two minutes, and then Ferguson and I immersed ourselves in our United memories. We relived great moments, laughed at less glorious episodes, and with a typical touch of Ferguson humour there was also room for the following remark: 'Peter, I have to consider the advantages of this matter: I won't have to argue with you all the time any more!' I think we continued in this vein for over half an hour, and I was late for training. But I was relieved. The decision had been made, there were plans for it to be announced, and in a year's time I would be starting a new life.

I had agreed with the management of the club that we would keep the news of my departure quiet. I was asked not to publicise my decision straight away, and we agreed that, if possible, we would try to find a time to air the matter that would suit both parties. I was very satisfied with this situation. I felt that by giving them such early notice, and by agreeing to keep things under wraps for a while, I had lived up to the club's standards for proper behaviour. It also meant that the club had ample time to study the goalkeeping market and find a replacement. I also emphasised the fact that I would not start to make concrete decisions about my future until the season was over. Ferguson and I shook hands on a promise that we would be loyal to each other no matter what happened, and we both kept to that.

As it turned out, I was to find myself in need of Ferguson's unconditional support that autumn when I suffered from a lack of form. I don't think I played badly, but I made a number of uncharacteristic mistakes, and it didn't go unnoticed. It was not a particularly pleasant situation to be in, but it didn't affect me that much, even though the English and Danish media seemed agreed about the fact that I was finished as a footballer and that I would soon find myself on the bench. Their predictions were put to the sword by Ferguson, who backed me up through thick and thin and never had the slightest intention of leaving me out of the side. And as it turned out, viewed in the light of the season as a whole, I guess it proved to be a sensible policy.

On the plus side, I finally got a little bit of holiday, and that was something I was badly in need of after the World Cup and almost three years without a break. Ferguson gave me a couple of weeks off, and I took my family with me to Barbados, where I had the dubious pleasure for the first time in my life of being hounded by the so-called paparazzi. I never met them face to face, of course; that is not usually their way of working. In fact, I wasn't even aware of their presence until I saw a picture of myself in swimming trunks filling the back page of the *Sun*, which was naturally on sale on the island. It felt a bit like having a burglar in the house. From the angle of the picture I figured out that it must have been taken from out at sea, so I concluded that the lousy photographers must simply have been lying in wait out on a boat.

This experience only served to convince me that I had made the right decision about leaving United. I was becoming rather tired of all the public commitments that are part and parcel of the job of playing for one of the biggest clubs in the world, a club which at the same time is a giant business where the media play a decisive role. For a long time I'd had the feeling that I wasn't playing for a football team, but was more a member of a giant rock 'n' roll band on a never-ending world tour. We were under constant surveillance, and with the way things were developing at United it was only a question of time before the club acquired its own TV station. MUTV, or Manchester United Television, made its debut in the autumn of 1998.

I quickly realised what this would involve for the players.

We were expected to be available for the cameras every day after training, which would of course have been OK if it was limited to that. But if you talked to MUTV, your words would certainly be quoted widely in the media the following day, in addition to which the interview would be shown on Sky Sports, because Sky Sports owns a third of MUTV. I felt that I was completely losing control with regard to how and where I was being quoted. When you are in contact with the media to such an extent, it is vitally important to be in control of what you say and to whom, but with MUTV as a link this control vanished into thin air. Furthermore, you don't need a degree to predict that one interview after training would quickly become insufficient for a channel which broadcasts four hours a day solely about Manchester United.

As I mentioned, there was a lot of criticism of me during the autumn of 1998, and this gave rise to a host of rumours concerning my future. It was in order to stop these rumours and to pre-empt further speculation that on 12 November we chose to make a public statement concerning my plans for the future. We would have preferred to wait until March 1999, but sometimes there are things which are difficult to control the way you would like to.

We called a press conference, and it turned out to be a bit of an occasion. It was a little bewildering, really, because there was very little I could say. I could only confirm that I would be leaving the club at the end of the season and that my plans for the future were not settled. And that was an overstatement, because I hadn't even started to think about how my career would pan out after leaving Old Trafford.

The thing that had worried me most beforehand was how the club's fans would react to the news. They are the bedrock of the club, and together with TV they provide the financial basis for the existence of the club and its players. But Alex Ferguson had reassured me in advance: 'You mark my words. You won't have any problems. On the contrary. There's nothing to worry about.' And he was right. No one talked about desertion. No one begrudged me my decision. In fact, I sensed a warmth which flowed towards me from all sides, and which confirmed two things for me: that Manchester United have the best fans in the world, and that my last season was going to be a big one. Very big.

And this turned out to be true, of course. After losing 2–3 to Middlesbrough at Old Trafford on 19 December 1998, United started a unique run of 34 games without defeat which enabled us to land the Treble. This run included a number of nerve-racking duels which without a doubt ensured that my last season was a very special experience.

There can be few readers, and for that matter few footballers, in this world who can really know the kind of pressure that is put on a club involved in the decisive stages of three of the most important competitions in the world. The Premier League, the FA Cup and the Champions' League inevitably involve the most closely matched showdowns where ultimately it is the will to win, and not necessarily the best play, which decides the outcome.

Looking back, there were a number of games towards the end of the season I am extremely proud to have had the chance to take part in – first and foremost because we won them, but also because they turned out to be fine advertisements for the most beautiful game of all. Of course, it would be difficult for me to describe all the games in our undefeated run, but, if I am going to make a selection, then the two FA Cup semi-final games against Arsenal rank very high on my list of memorable confrontations. In addition to the fact that United and Arsenal fought neck and neck in the race for the Premiership title, there is always a very unique atmosphere surrounding the FA Cup. Every team gives their utmost in order to reach Wembley, and that was certainly the case in those two dramatic matches played on a neutral ground.

Villa Park was bursting at the seams for the two games. They were played at a breathtaking pace, the kind of pace you only find in British football. To an unrelenting tempo both Arsenal and United attempted to outdo each other by scoring that single goal which often makes the difference when the two best defences in the land go head to head.

In the first encounter on 11 April we actually succeeded in

scoring a great goal, but to our astonishment the linesman chose to flag for offside. Giggs, after an overlap on the left, embarked on a long run down towards the goal line, where at that precise moment Dwight Yorke was in an offside position. With his perfect poise, Giggs sent a high-flying cross into the box which grazed the heads of the defenders and landed right at the feet of Roy Keane, who drove the ball into the net with a perfect half-volley. At that instant I was certain the game had been decided in our favour, and I was both disappointed and angry when I realised that the referee insisted on following an interpretation of the laws that was, to put it mildly, debatable. In fact, it was clearly a blunder. Giggs had moved the ball forward while retaining possession, and when that happens there is no way that anyone in front of the ball can be penalised for being in an offside position. The linesman can be excused for the error because he did not have the necessary overall view of the game, but I believe the referee – David Elleray – had no justification whatsoever for his actions.

This contentious ruling became the subject of a heated debate during the days that followed, and it was regrettable because it would have suited us perfectly to have come out of that gruelling game with a win. Four days previously we had drawn 1–1 with Juventus in the first leg of the semi-final of the European Cup at Old Trafford, and now we had to face yet another game against Arsenal with only three days' break.

Once again the venue was Villa Park, and once again it was the same referee – and the same linesmen. It could have been a bad omen, but this replay also turned out to be a dramatic and exciting football match, with an unbelievable conclusion. Roy Keane was sent off just as Arsenal had equalised our lead, so we had to play the rest of the game with ten men. All the same, we held Arsenal at 1–1 until the last minute of ordinary time, when the Gunners – after having just had a goal disallowed – were quite fairly awarded a penalty.

I had more or less lost my sense of time and was under the impression that there were at least seven or eight minutes of the game left, so as Dennis Bergkamp placed the ball on the spot the full implications of the penalty kick hadn't really hit me. Looking back on it now, I can see that at that point I was facing one of the most important moments of my career with United. If Bergkamp had scored, we would have been knocked out of the cup. And if that had been the case, I don't think we could have gone on to win the Premiership. But none of this was on my mind at the time. I was only thinking about saving the penalty.

Being a goalkeeper facing a penalty is a bit like boxing against an opponent who is two weight classes above you: you don't have much chance of winning. And if you want to win, you have to take a chance; gamble on the outcome, choose red or black, odd or even. I gambled correctly and hit the jackpot. The Wembley dream was still alive.

That knocked the stuffing out of Arsenal, and in extra time Giggs scored perhaps one of the most beautiful goals of his career, which is saying a lot. It was a fantastic sight from my position in goal. He snapped up the ball around the halfway line, then started to accelerate. He had four or five men in front of him, but he ran on with the intention of weaving himself in and out of what is unquestionably the best defence in England. I could see that the running of our two frontmen was creating sufficient confusion in Arsenal's defence to open up the room Giggs needed to work in. He went past the first man, then the second and the third, and from a sharp angle on the left he hammered the ball high over the head of David Seaman and into the roof of the net.

I knew the game was all over after that. Arsenal didn't have anything left in the locker. Once more our enormous reserves of mental strength had won the day.

After that nerve-racking and exhausting match we had three days before we had to face Sheffield Wednesday at home. That proved to be unproblematic: we won 3–0 and were then ready to leave for Italy, where we were to meet Juventus four days later in the second leg of the European Cup semi-final.

This was another momentous occasion. In the first match at Old Trafford on 7 April, Juventus had played really well, dominating the midfield and putting us under enormous pressure. Ryan Giggs had got us out of trouble, but there was no doubt that Juventus had the edge on us in Turin thanks to that away goal.

From our earlier experiences we should have had reason to fear the Italians. They had knocked us out of the Champions' League before, but the attitude of the team was one of great calm and a high degree of confidence. We were aware that we had to take the initiative, and we were quite sure we could do it.

Most important of all, we knew *how* we had to do it.

All the same, with only ten minutes of the game gone, the scoreboard showed Juventus ahead 2–0. Still, we had a good rhythm to our game; we had the majority of the possession; and we felt comfortable. The fact that Filippo Inzaghi had latched on to a whipped cross into the area after only six minutes, and four minutes later had grabbed another, one of those strange goals where a foot gets in the way and totally changes the direction of the ball, was not enough to knock us completely off our feet. Naturally I was annoyed at conceding the two goals. But at the same time I was confident that we would be able to change the course of the game.

After only 24 minutes' play, Roy Keane signalled a change of fortunes. Keane's energy is incredible. He rose in front of two Italians at the near post following a corner on the left. As if it was the most natural thing in the world, he directed the ball powerfully into the opposite side of the goal. The flabbergasted Italians just stood and watched. I believe that goal didn't just tilt the balance of the game in our favour – it cracked the Italians psychologically. They could feel us breathing down their necks, and they knew it was only a question of time before we would equalise. And that would mean we would take over the game completely.

Ten minutes later the fate of the Italians was sealed. It was a spectacular goal, designed and executed by our two spearheads, 'the twins', Andy Cole and Dwight Yorke. Cole received a long pass well out on the right side of the Italian half, and immediately – with that in-built radar he has for where his mate's positioned – sent the ball hard into the

Italian penalty area, perfectly placed between the two defenders in the box. Yorke came flying in and headed the ball precisely and firmly past the Italian goalkeeper, Angelo Peruzzi.

The Italian fans in the crowd were dumbfounded, as were the Italian players. The game had crumbled in their hands. They had thrown away what appeared to them to be a comfortable lead. Now it was United who were ahead on the away-goal rule. We were on our way to the final, and from this point the confrontation took its logical and unrelenting course. Towards the end of the game, in a disorganised attempt by the Italians to get back into the match, the Juventus defenders were once more overrun by our front duo. In the 80th minute Yorke broke through in the middle and was brought down, but before the referee could blow his whistle for the penalty, Cole had already coolly put the loose ball home to seal a stunning 3–2 victory.

The last game I want to recall is the final match of the Premiership season. The task was simple: we had to beat Tottenham at Old Trafford to make sure that Arsenal couldn't pass us in the race for the title. It was Sunday, 16 May, and the United team that ran out on to the pitch had already secured a place in two finals and was now in a position, for the first time in my career, to clinch the championship in front of the home crowd.

Perhaps that was the reason we got off to a nervous start. We not only wasted some clear-cut chances, but suddenly found ourselves a goal behind thanks to what I would call a give-away goal. It was not a comfortable situation. The game seemed to be slipping away, and the pressure from our fans with their enormous expectations was hard to bear. And then, at last, the United machine started to roll. We knew we'd be unstoppable when, just before half-time, David Beckham blasted one of his trademark goals into the top corner.

Just after the break it was Andy Cole who weaved his magic when, under pressure in the Spurs penalty area, he received the ball, brought it under control and lobbed it over the on-rushing goalkeeper. Then all he had to do was wait for the roar of the 55,000 fans as the ball sailed into the net. After that it was just a matter of passing time until the referee could blow his whistle. United's fifth championship title of the 1990s was a reality.

At the finish, there were scenes of overwhelming jubilation. Old Trafford swayed backward and forward almost dangerously, and for the players the experience of clinching the title at home was almost like doing it for the first time. It was at this point that it really dawned on me that I had just played my last game for Manchester United at Old Trafford. But in the hour of victory there was no room for sentimentality, and I managed pretty well to get through my farewell speech to the fans, scheduled as a part of that final game.

My children, Kasper and Cecilie, joined me on the pitch. I walked around the ground hand in hand with them, waving to the fans, and I couldn't help thinking back to that little silver-haired boy from Gladsaxe in Denmark, who had dreamed about just such a day.

3 Early Days in Denmark

'I can pinpoint precisely the date of the first match I ever played in. It was on 7 August 1972, the day before my youngest sister, Hanne, was born. My mother has told me – I don't remember it myself – that she was packing her bag and was ready to leave for the hospital, but that she managed to find the time to go and watch me make my debut.'

M Y FATHER IS POLISH. My mother had a job as a child's nurse on an immigrants' ship. The ship docked in the Polish town of Gybnia and she went ashore for a short holiday in the nearby seaside resort of Sopot. Here she met my father and after several more visits to Poland they got married in 1961. They soon had the opportunity to settle in Denmark, something they both welcomed.

Since my father is Polish, my two oldest sisters and I were born with his nationality. The three of us received Danish citizenship in 1970.

I was my parents' second child and first son when I first saw the light of day on 18 November 1963. The first few years of my life were spent in Buddinge, a suburb of Copenhagen, where the family home was.

The earliest childhood memory I have has nothing whatsoever to do with football: it was a plane trip from Copenhagen to the city of Aalborg in the north of Jutland. Every summer – in fact, every single summer for about ten years – my sisters and I went to stay with my grandparents for a fortnight's summer holiday, followed by another week with my mother's aunt. It was an established routine which brought us into contact with a mildly religious evangelicalism in the town of Thisted, in a district of Denmark called Thy. But no one ever tried to indoctrinate us in any way, and we weren't influenced by it at all. In fact, we enjoyed our freedom and its little luxuries: we were given plenty of roast pork with home-made gravy and all kinds of fruit and vegetables from a huge kitchen garden, while we played games with some of the local children, who were a bit curious about 'the kids from Copenhagen'. My first impression of the Thy area was that it was a very big place set in a vast natural landscape under wide open skies, but later on I realised that Thisted was perhaps not so enormous after all.

On the last holiday I took there I didn't really think much about the wide open skies and the plentiful space to play in. That summer I was more concerned about whether I would ever run out on to a football pitch again. During the weeks leading up to our annual Thisted vacation, I had been in bed with flu-like symptoms. In the last week I had particularly acute pains in my hip and the night-duty doctor was sent for on several occasions. My mother was working night shifts that week and so I was home alone. When she returned from duty on the night before our departure for Jutland, she found me in agony and immediately took me to hospital. I was examined and X-rayed but the doctors couldn't really come up with any answers. They wanted to admit me but I was desperate to go on holiday and fought them all the way. In the end I was allowed to go, promising to return to hospital as soon as I got back to Copenhagen. As it turned out, on the holiday I was forced to lie on a sofa for three weeks, hardly able to move. On two occasions the night-duty doctor was called. He thought the best thing would be for me to be admitted to Thisted Hospital. I wasn't going to spend the last days of my holiday in hospital! I was quite sure about that! I said I would rather limp about with my mother's aunt's old stick.

On the day of our return I was suddenly well again. No pains in my hip, no headache, no fever. Relieved and happy, we headed for Copenhagen and considered our appointment at the hospital the next day a mere formality. It came as quite a shock when I was admitted immediately. The results of some blood tests showed I had a serious infection. There was nothing else to do than to keep me there.

I was told to lie still in bed since there was a risk that the infection would spread to my entire body if I ran around. This wasn't great news for a wild kid of fifteen and it seemed the torment was endless. Weeks came and went and the doctors couldn't agree on what was wrong with me and what treatment to give me.

I sensed my mother's concern. She was a trained nurse so she was accustomed to observing prolonged illness, but she grew more and more nervous. After three weeks an operation was scheduled and the doctors found their answers. I had an infection in the hip that required treatment with antibiotics. It all amounted to five weeks in the hospital and six months without football. It's hard to say which was the most difficult to bear. But the experience certainly taught be to be grateful for the ability to move around freely, something we take for granted.

For most of my childhood we lived in the Copenhagen suburb of Hoje-Gladsaxe. This is the place I regard as my real childhood home. Our family life was a little peculiar since both my mother and father had jobs that involved working at night. My father was a musician. Every evening in the summer season he played from seven to eleven o'clock at the Nimb restaurant in the Tivoli Gardens in Copenhagen, and afterwards at a bar called Alotria from midnight until five o'clock in the morning. My mother was a nurse at the State University Hospital and was on night duty every other week.

When my mother was working we children looked after ourselves and each other. Hardly a lifestyle that would be practicable today – not in my home anyway. But back then things were different. We were never truly alone anyway since we had friendly neighbours all around. We knew we could turn to them with even the smallest problem, and we could always call our mother. I think that if you were to ask my mother's former colleagues, they would remember us as the children who always called to rat on each other: 'Mum, Peter is teasing us.' I used to tease my sisters quite a lot. Then I would get a call from my mother and was told to behave myself. My improved behaviour rarely lasted long, though, and then my sisters would have to call again!

The fact that I was a bit of a tearaway as a child is no secret. I quickly developed into a big lad and I loved all kinds of physical challenges, whether they presented themselves on the pitch or in the form of outdoor activities. I remember quite clearly once how I, together with several other fearless types, discovered a number of slopes behind the block of flats where we lived, where with the right kind of run-up it was possible to launch yourself into the air. The challenge was – naturally – who could jump the greatest distance. The best leaps were probably about 30 feet in length, and these weren't without a certain element of danger. I can clearly see that today, but none of the boys ever hurt himself badly. Of course we got a few knocks – that was par for the course – but we just picked ourselves up again and planned the next jump, the one we hoped would set a new record.

This emphasis on physical activity, where everything was done at a running pace, meant that most of the time I had a hard time sitting still in school. Not that I was a real trouble-maker, but I did experience more problems with teachers and headmasters than most children. I was a bit cheeky, mostly in the time-honoured way. We had to see who could play up the most without things getting completely out of hand.

There is no doubt in my mind that football helped to shape my character from quite an early age. The discipline alone required to play in a team, combined with three evenings of training every week plus a match at the weekend, meant that the game occupied a lot of my time. I can pinpoint precisely the date of the first match I ever played in. It was 7 August 1972, the day before my youngest sister, Hanne, was born. My mother has told me – I don't remember it myself – that she was packing her bag and was ready to leave for the hospital, but that she managed to find the time to go and watch me make my debut. If it hadn't been for the bushes that surrounded the pitch, she would actually have been able to follow my first efforts from our kitchen window.

I can't remember the results of my first games either. I can only say that I played for the local club, Hoje-Gladsaxe, and I started my career as a goalkeeper, like a duck to water. I don't even think there was any discussion about it, although it is possible that the coach thought it was probably the safest thing to do, to put the little wild kid in goal. However it happened, it was good for me because I wasn't quite so hot with my feet.

Almost from my very first match the seeds of achieving something great in the world of football were sown. People, and I mean adult people, started to say to me: 'You'll end up playing for Denmark!' And I was nine years old! I didn't think I was especially good, but looking back I can see that I had a certain kind of mentality – an ability to concentrate, a determination to channel my efforts – already in place at that time, which probably made all the difference. And one of my driving forces from those early days on was the fact that I didn't want to let down all those adults around me who had voiced such great expectations.

I was headhunted after a two-and-a-half-year unbeaten run when I was still a boy. I was approached by a much bigger club, Hero, which had one of Denmark's largest youth schemes. With another team-mate – Peter K. Nielsen, the most promising football talent I have ever seen – I was almost enticed into joining the club, which was quite a common thing in those days. Hero was in a much better league than Hoje-Gladsaxe and the players at the club mostly came from the suburb of Hoje-Gladsaxe anyway. I knew most of the kids from school so the change was the most natural thing in the world for me.

Hero held much bigger adventures, too. On occasion, one of the club's teams would play a warm-up match before AB's home games. At the time AB were in the First Division and were one of the best teams in the country. So it was quite an experience to get to play at Gladsaxe Stadium in front of a crowd larger than we had in a whole season.

We also managed to get to the Copenhagen Football Association Cup final, which was played at the fantastic national stadium. This final was my first appearance at 'The Park'. It was a euphoric experience. We played against KB, whose team included Michael Laudrup and Torben Piechnik as 'the big names'. It's still a little humiliating to admit that we actually lost 3–4 (even then, I hated to lose), but the defeat in no way erased the joy and pride I felt at having played at the Danish national stadium.

When Gladsaxe and Hero merged to form Gladsaxe-Hero Football Club, it became a Zealand Football Association club. This meant that we were up against teams from other areas of the country. The Copenhagen FA would automatically have chosen several of us for representative sides had the merger not taken place. As it was, it took many years for the Zealand FA to get around to selecting us.

Representative teams are the foundation of the Danish FA Youth National Team. If you are not on a selected team, the chances of breaking into the Youth National Team are slim. Clubs nominate players who attend trials for selection for the association teams. Gladsaxe-Hero was very slow in nominating players. When they finally got round to it, as many as five players from our year group were selected for the Zealand FA junior team. I was seventeen years old when I was selected. It was the first time I had had the opportunity to play for a team composed of the very best players in the area. I graduated to the senior squad, and at that time I met a man who was destined to play an important role in my life. That man was Svend Aage Hansen, who was the coach for Gladsaxe-Hero's first team in the Third Division. That season the team was relegated to the Danish National League, a situation which was already unavoidable with three games left to play. As the youth team had finished at the top of its league, Hansen took the brave decision to promote seven players from the youth team. That was my debut in a Danish league team. It was against Birkerod and we lost 1–0, but I remember that I played well and was mentioned in a couple of newspapers. The defeat didn't mean anything anyway as the club was already destined for the drop.

But Svend Aage – who, by the way, later became my father-in-law – obviously had a plan. The team that was to play in the Danish National League the following season needed fresh blood and consistency in selection. He thought that I should be a part of his side, but he was also convinced that I should only stay with the club for two more seasons. Then I should make a move to Hvidovre's First Division side. After that I was to play for Denmark. And, finally, I was to have a professional career abroad.

When he outlined this to me he made quite an impression on a lad who hadn't yet turned eighteen, and who hadn't really been thinking in quite those terms. I admit that I had been approached by B1903 who wanted me to play on their youth team, but I wasn't really interested in that offer. The club seemed a bit boring to me. On the other hand, the idea of joining Hvidovre excited me. They wore red shirts and blue shorts, and they had just played Juventus, and that was something else!

Svend Aage – nicknamed 'Skinny' – put his plan into action. He split the youth team up completely, and eight of us, with Christian Andersen as sweeper and two other veterans, formed the team that was to play for the season. It didn't go quite as well as he had expected, but it was an extremely exciting season. In the last game we had to face Stubbekobing away from home, needing only one point to avoid relegation. Stubbekobing had to win to stay up. In that game, Svend Aage made one of those tactical moves which proves to be a masterpiece. He decided that he would give one of my really good friends, Henrik Loften, his debut. Loften had experienced some problems with the junior team coach (he was still a junior at the time) which had led to a parting of ways. But he was so talented that Svend Aage had picked him in the starting line-up for this extremely important game. After only eleven minutes Loften repaid the trust in him by giving us the lead.

We won the game and I remember playing as well as I had ever done. More importantly, we avoided relegation. It was a good job that we did because we were not the most popular team at the club – Svend Aage had picked so many young players for the first team that we all encountered a great deal of animosity from certain senior players, particularly those who had been left out.

If Gladsaxe-Hero had been relegated it would have been a catastrophe, but the thing I remember best about that day was when Svend Aage's daughter, Bente, who had watched the majority of our games that season, came rushing on to the pitch after the game and gave me a tremendous hug. I was the hero of the day. And from that day we started to go out with each other. In the end, we got married.

But that's jumping ahead of things a bit. It might be hard to believe, but I did find time for things other than football, even though it demanded a carefully planned schedule. At one point I lived in Smorumnedre, which is further outside Copenhagen, went to school in Rodovre, nearer the centre of the city, and played football in Gladsaxe. In order to get everything organised, I developed a comprehensive knowledge of the bus and train timetables in the Copenhagen area. It is no exaggeration when I say that at that point in my life I knew the departure times of all trains and buses, not just from Ballerup station, but also from Gladsaxe Terminal, Jyllingevej station and Islev. Within a matter of seconds I could work out the best connections at more or less any time of the day or night, and even though this may sound a touch obsessive, it certainly saved me a lot of time.

My dedication to the timetables might, perhaps, have had something to do with the fact that for the first time ever in my life I had started to enjoy going to school. After having been virtually thrown out of the local school in Smorumnedre, where I had a slight confrontation with our religious studies teacher about the disproportionate amount of time spent on the subject of Islam, my mother encouraged me to apply for enrolment at the National Innovation Centre for General Education in Rodovre. This turned out to be a fantastic school with a low teacher/pupil ratio, and it gave the whole idea of going to school a new meaning for me. Learning suddenly became interesting, new worlds opened themselves to me, and the school showed a certain amount of consideration to my involvement in football. Suddenly it became possible to combine things, and that was mostly thanks to my class tutor, Ib O. Petersen, who was also the head teacher.

He was genuinely fascinated by my footballing activities, showing real interest and always mentioning it on a Monday morning: 'I see you drew 2–2,' that kind of thing. He showed me a completely new kind of understanding and, as we also got on very well together, he was very important for me. He taught me the meaning of freedom with responsibility, and at the same time he was very strict with me when, in spite of all my efforts, I got into minor difficulties. I felt that he showed a special interest in me, and I had three fantastic years at that school. Last year I received the sad news that Ib had passed away. He was the one person in the world that I least wanted to disappoint. He taught me the values of life and how to live by them. He taught me to respect other people. He taught me to respect myself. And he taught me to allow time for things other than football. Right up until his death I had stayed in touch with Ib. He was one of the finest men I have ever met. The world has become a poorer place in his absence.

Apart from football and school, I also paid attention to my, if not glorious, then at least fairly extensive portfolio of jobs, which has included everything from collecting recyclable bottles at the local supermarket and working in factories and offices to laying floors and selling advertising space, until I reached my final goal: full-time professional footballer. I am happy to be in a position to say that I have never regretted any of it. The jobs I had were widely different in content and character, but they equipped me with a considerable amount of human and social insight which I wouldn't have been without.

It may not sound very convincing when I say that it was great fun working in the dyeing department of a textile factory, but I really thought it was. Getting to know about the many different processes was really interesting and challenging, although they were perhaps not quite as complicated as you might imagine. We worked with highly dangerous chemicals, so the job required full concentration during operation. If we happened to get the chemicals on our fingers, we had to rub our hands in a special powder. This powder was so potent that it ignited if you dropped some of it on the floor. At the factory not enough attention was paid to safety regulations, and I have to admit that in the end I became so concerned that I handed in my notice.

But I had to earn some money, so I took a cleaning job at an old people's home. That wasn't a bad job at all. We started work at seven o'clock in the morning, were finished by midday, and the money was fine. I didn't need much cash at that time. I actually stuck with that job for a whole year, but those twelve months were long enough.

The next thing I tried was a real office job, with the World Wildlife Fund. Originally I was given a job helping out in the stores and the shop, but after I had been there for three weeks the shop manager resigned, and suddenly I was promoted to sales manager. It was a very interesting place to work and I learned a lot during that time.

Shortly afterwards I was called up by the defence department to do my four-week military service. Of course, the WWF gave me the time off. But matters got really complicated because at the same time I had started playing for Hvidovre and was requested to attend a training camp in Portugal. The situation with the defence department and the WWF got rather delicate until I was permitted to go to Portugal so long as I finished by military service the following month. That gave me a fortnight at the WWF on my return from the training camp. During those two weeks I realised that office work and Peter Schmeichel probably didn't have the brightest future together.

So I quit my job and my father-in-law offered me an apprenticeship in his flooring firm. This proposal came at the right time, and it was certainly a completely different type of job. It was really hard work crawling around on floors all day, and the bigger jobs were also complicated. Laying 10,000 square feet of lino is not easy. In fact, it's quite a complex mathematical jigsaw puzzle, where all the pieces have to fit in the end. We worked, for example, at the government defence headquarters, and several times at Vestre prison in Copenhagen. Seeing what I saw on those jobs in the prison gave me an even greater aversion to all types of crime. My career as a floor layer ended when I discovered that my knees just couldn't take it. As an adult I have always weighed between fourteen and a half and fifteen and a half stones, and my knees just couldn't stand the strain.

My last job outside football was the one I had just after I stopped laying floors. By this time I was playing for Hvidovre, and the chairman of the club, Niels Erik Madsen, offered me a job as an advertising consultant with a newspaper in

Hvidovre, which he owned. That was great fun! I made a lot of contacts, there were plenty of laughs, and working conditions were flexible, which allowed me more or less to plan my work as I wanted to.

A couple of months later, in the Spring of 1987, I received a call from Brondby football club, asking if I would be interested in signing for them.

4 Brondby

'Morten Olsen suddenly shouted as he tore three of
four sheets off the clipboard: "You're professionals!
Money is important to you!" And when I looked at the
clipboard, hanging on it were twenty 1,000-kroner
notes neatly arranged in two fan shapes. "This is also
what you're playing for tonight. If we go on to the next
round, this is your bonus." Now 20,000 kroner is a lot
of money (nearly £2,000), and the sight of it really
opened people's eyes.'

L ET'S FACE IT, football is about people and money. While money is vital in developing a team, just as important is having the right people at the right time at all levels of the club, inside and out. Brondby, who I helped win the Danish championship in 1987, 1988, 1990 and 1991 (we had to make do with winning the cup in 1989), was a superb example of how these two factors can gel to great effect. And when I tell people about the time I spent at the club I find it only natural to see things from that point of view.

When I arrived at Brondby in the spring of 1987, I naturally had an ambition to become Denmark's number one goalkeeper, and to get thoroughly acquainted with the European elite at club level. The club wasn't quite ready for this level of competition when I joined – even though results were good – and when coach Ebbe Skovdahl left us for Benfica and Birger Peitersen arrived in his place, the club's prospects did not improve. Peitersen was an entirely different kind of trainer altogether. He regarded the team as *his* team, but you don't have to be at Brondby long to realise that Brondby is not one man's team but everybody's team. It has to do with the culture that permeates the club, which doesn't respect personal interests and ambitions. Above all, the club is a family club, built around voluntary leadership, usually that of the parents of children who play there. The involvement of so many people from different walks of life is overwhelming, and as a player or manager you need to realise that you are no more important than the person standing next to you.

It's probably not a bad idea to discard all your prejudices when you go to a club like Brondby. I certainly learnt that pretty quickly. My preconceptions of the club were based on outside knowledge, and I must admit that as a result I thought the players on the team would be tough and uncompromising. The exact opposite turned out to be true. It was probably the most close-knit group I've ever been a part of. It was almost impossible to feel excluded because friendliness prevailed and people took such good care of each other. It's quite normal, for instance, for football teams to play cards, and almost just as inevitable that this activity will lead to the formation of cliques. But it wasn't like that at Brondby. If you sat down and said you wanted to be in on the next round then, well, you were in on the next round. This natural openness was one of the greatest things about the club.

Of course it helped that we travelled a lot as a team, because spending so much time together sharpens your awareness of what kind of behaviour is acceptable. It was actually pretty incredible how nice and harmonious it was, and most incredible of all was the fact that no one person made all the decisions. Lars Olsen was our captain, but he was not the kind of guy who was particularly keen on ruling the roost off the pitch. The team was the sum of a mass of personalities and, of course, the subject of no end of discussions. But these talks only helped to emphasise how well we stuck together, and made life around the team tremendously exciting.

It is unavoidable that during training and in certain other situations squabbles will always break out, and occasionally these will end in a fight. But the difference at Brondby was that everything was forgiven and forgotten by the time the players were sitting in the changing room.

The team's focus was to a large extent dominated by the objective of winning championships, something we managed to do on a fairly regular basis. Apart from that, what was most important to us was to play good football and to have fun, first and foremost on the pitch, then after the games.

Not only did the players and management form a close-knit unit, our wives and girlfriends also contributed a lot to the overall sense of cohesion – which, by the way, is as solid today as it was then. The support they gave us has always been grossly underestimated. I would go so far as to say that had they not been there – had they largely minded their own business and taken care of the home and the children – we could never have achieved the results we did. This certainly applied to me. My respect and gratitude for this support does not diminish when I think of how we lived our lives in those days. After practically every match the players went into town, not just one or two of us but the whole team. I'm not quite sure whether this was accepted without any complaints at all, but broadly speaking it was accepted. I'm pretty sure it doesn't work quite that way today. It may sound strange, but I'm convinced that those nights we spent together after the games were a vital element of our success. We inevitably talked about football, and many things were dealt with before they became a problem. We also got to know each other, our families and personal circumstances pretty well, and that helped a lot.

Skovdahl returned briefly from Benfica to replace Birger Peitersen, and then it was Morten Olsen's turn to work with the team. The season when Brondby became serious contenders in top-flight European football was 1990/91, and this was achieved by means of Morten Olsen's well-known methods, a combination of grit and robot-like discipline that put most of us in excellent physical condition, something for which we should still be grateful to him.

I remember that first training session under Olsen. We started the day with a glass of champagne, which we drank standing there in our tracksuits. Then we went on what we thought was a really long run through the woods. When we got to the dyke, though, and expected to head back to the stadium, we were directed along some woodland paths and out towards to the beach, which was actually quite a long way. When we got back, Morten said, 'I'm easing you in gently today.' He was spot-on. His physical training routine got more and more demanding. Sometimes a fortnight would go by without our playing football at all. To begin with there were quite a few strain injuries, but as people got more robust and strong these became far less common. It's horrendous now to think what we went through, but it was so exciting at the time. And since Morten Olsen was always ahead of the field, quite a few of us thought: 'I'll be damned if I can't do that too.' When the basics were over and done with, most of us noticed what an enormous pleasure it had become to play football. We had become so much stronger than our opponents. That was a really good feeling.

Quite a few players flourished and excelled themselves under the regime. People like Erik Rasmussen and Carsten V. Jensen achieved high international standards, and it was this kind of progress we capitalised on when the Brondby machine really got into full swing. One man who only really got into shape under Morten, and a crucial element of Olsen's grand plan, was Usche. Usche came to Brondby as a partner for Friday Ellahore, who was supposed to be a real star – the new Brian Laudrup and all that. In fact it turned out that Brondby was more interested in buying Usche, but he would only come to Denmark if Friday came too, so the club bought him as well.

Brondby had a fairy-tale run in the 1990/91 UEFA Cup competition, with Morten as coach. It started with a sensational 5–0 victory over Eintracht Frankfurt at Copenhagen's old stadium, and a slightly less brilliant, and pretty traumatic, 4–1 defeat at their home ground in the return match. But we were already into the next round, and one by one we despatched Ferencvaros of Hungary, Bayer Leverkusen and Torpedo Moscow, until we faced the most prestigious showdown in Brondby's history, the semi-final match against AC Roma. We had drawn at home 0–0, but the return match in Rome developed into a game of high drama in which we were only seconds from a place in the final. Unfortunately, that wily German goal poacher Rudi Voller managed to shatter our dreams with a goal just before the referee blew the final whistle. A bitter pill to swallow, no doubt about that, but in retrospect we could be proud of our efforts all the same. The run emphasised Brondby's international class, and it's one reason why today Brondby is a name people respect. That match was also my final major game with Brondby before I went to join Manchester United.

Not long after I left, Morten Olsen got the sack. There's no denying that his style was rather autocratic and dictatorial, and he's been fired from other European clubs for the same reason. What happens is that tolerance of him and his style fades away when things start to go wrong. There are no problems as long as he's successful, but his attitude makes him vulnerable when the results fail to materialise. As a trainer you naturally have to stick to your principles and not let anyone take advantage of you, but it's never a bad idea to listen to your physio when he says, 'The players' legs are falling off.' You can't ignore that kind of thing. But I think – it was his first position as a trainer, after all – that Morten was quite simply afraid that the team wouldn't get into good enough shape. And it's all too easy to push people just that little bit too far.

I was always 100 per cent satisfied with Morten as trainer. He was exactly what I needed at that stage of my career in my struggle to get on. I can't say I enjoyed it, but his physical training gave me a platform I've been able to build on ever since. Anyone can send a team off running, but getting the dosage right is vital. Morten's great strength was his ability to motivate us, keep us up to scratch so that we didn't stagnate. I'm convinced that the group of players he inherited was extremely amenable to his style. This was a crucial ingredient in the success he enjoyed at Brondby.

One example of his unorthodox way of getting us going occurred before the home leg with Bayer Leverkusen in the third round of the UEFA Cup. At the tactics meeting that morning he went over the usual stuff, and the players always listened to what the man had to say – well, sort of. Once in a while you found your thoughts drifting out through the windows of the Hotel Marina, where the view of the sea was always captivating, and you tended to lose concentration a bit. Morten was quite aware of that, I reckon, because he suddenly shouted as he tore three or four sheets off the clipboard: 'You're professionals! Money is important to you!' And when I looked at the clipboard, hanging on it were twenty 1,000-kroner notes neatly arranged in two fan shapes. 'This is also what you're playing for tonight. If we go on to the next round, this is your bonus.'

Now 20,000 kroner is a lot of money (nearly £2,000), and the sight of it really opened people's eyes. We later won the match 3–0. Whether it was the money that did it I'm not sure, but the way in which the message about how important the match was for us all was delivered has become a central part of the Brondby players' folklore. In fact the bonus wasn't 20,000 kroner, it was quite a bit less. And when the club brought this to Morten's attention, he said: 'Then I'll pay the difference myself.' We did go on to the next round, and the club coughed up the money.

Apart from his constant anxiety over our state of fitness, another of Morton's weaknesses was that he found it very difficult to let players sit on the sidelines. It's actually quite an art as a manager to hit a balance between the physio's opinion, the players' own perceptions and your own desire to turn out the best team possible. I think that as a trainer you have got to be able to listen and delegate responsibility. If someone is having problems, it's important not to take chances.

It's impossible for me to write about Brondby without mentioning Per Bjerregaard, who in his unobtrusive but effective way was the prime mover in the club's fantastic development. I met him for the first time when I was negotiating a contract with Brondby, talks that took place in the friendliest, most reassuring atmosphere you can possibly imagine. But later on, when the conditions of my transfer to Manchester United were being sorted out, I came into much closer contact with Bjerregaard's business methods, and that was a different matter entirely. As far as I was concerned, Bjerregaard was intent on delaying the whole process, but on the other hand I recognised that in contractual terms he held the whip hand. So for that reason – fortunately, I must say – I have no quarrel with either Brondby or Bjerregaard. But that's not to say that I can't tell the story of the sequence of events that occurred during negotiations with Manchester United.

It was quite a long-drawn-out process in which the two parties had entirely different interests. I was, after all, on a four-year contract with Brondby, and at the time English clubs were showing the most interest I was only two years into that contract. For me, there was no doubt that I wanted to move to England, and that this was what I was destined to do. And I naively had the idea that this could be done relatively quickly. Morten Olsen wasn't exactly keen on my leaving Brondby. His strong feelings naturally influenced both the strategy and the pace Per Bjerregaard set for the negotiations. The result of this was that I moved to England a year later than I had expected to. There was no lack of interest from English clubs wishing to secure my services, but Bjerregaard was in a position to hold his own against all bids by demanding a price which Manchester United wasn't particularly interested in paying. One consequence of Bjerregaard's negotiating tactics was, for me at least, a pretty restless summer holiday, during which I literally did not know whether I was coming or going.

On 15 May we were scheduled to play an international match against England at Wembley. It was, by the way, Richard Moller Nielsen's first game as head coach of the Danish squad. My agent at that time, Rune Hauge, had lined up a number of interested parties, including Kenny Dalglish, who was there to represent Liverpool. The day before the match I received an offer from QPR, and before that both Newcastle and West Ham showed an interest. And Manchester United were still interested, of course. In all modesty I had a great match at Wembley – even though we lost 1–0 – which helped to draw the big fish closer to the bait.

When we arrived back in Denmark, Bjerregaard called me and said: 'Both Liverpool and Manchester United are now officially interested. Which one do you prefer?'

I had already decided to join Manchester United, of course, although I quite naturally also toyed with the idea of Liverpool, who at that time were winning rather more matches than United. But I had made up my mind, and told Bjerregaard I wanted to go to Manchester. We spoke to each other perhaps three or four times a day after that, but even so the process was hampered by a definite inertia which rather surprised me.

The holiday season duly arrived, and as nothing concrete

had been agreed I said to Bjerregaard: 'Look, I'm going on holiday now.'

'Okay, that's fine. We'll keep in touch. And I'll carry on negotiating,' he replied.

After that we arranged that I would check my answerphone every day – this was before the days of widespread mobile phones.

I spent ten days in Jutland with my family, but not one message was left on my answering machine. I was rather irritated by this. It didn't help me to relax. When I returned to training after the holiday I was feeling disappointed, but also stubborn. I decided I would not ask about any of the details; it was up to Bjerregaard to approach me. I had a feeling that I could risk losing out on something if I was too pushy.

Other sources – and they always exist when transfers are going on; a number of different people try to force themselves into the negotiations in the hope of making some money – told me that Bjerregaard and Brondby had demanded £1.2 million for me and Manchester United hadn't wanted to pay more than £900,000. This bit of information made me even more cautious, as I could see there was a risk of losing part of my share of the proceeds if there was a big discrepancy between the offers.

I played cool, and went to training and then for a massage. The first person I met there was Per Bjerregaard. We exchanged civilities, as you do in a situation like that, but he didn't say a word to me about United or any other club. I didn't mention the matter either. His reluctance to talk about the transfer made me consider my next move – if you're patient enough the opportunity always arises.

That opportunity came at a press conference on the Monday before we were to play our first European Cup match against Eintracht Frankfurt. I knew that Bjerregaard, who is from Jutland, read *Jyllands-Posten* (one of the major broadsheets) every morning. So when the paper's sports reporter, Jan Lund, asked me how the summer's negotiations had gone, I grabbed the opportunity. I explained the situation to him and asked if he would help me. He agreed, and wrote a brief story about the sequence of events in which it was to appear as though he had asked me for the details out of interest, whereas it was actually me who had given him the questions and answers. What I wanted the paper to say was that I felt that Brondby had deliberately delayed the proceedings by demanding too much money for me, and that the club had told me absolutely nothing since I returned to training.

The article, which wasn't much longer than a single paragraph, appeared in the paper on the day of the match, and ten seconds after the game was over, Bjerregaard appeared beside me – not to congratulate me on what had actually been a fine 5–0 victory, but to defend himself and Brondby against my claims. He denied that the club had demanded £1.2 million for me, but Martin Edwards, the chairman of Manchester United, has since confirmed that figure for me, so there must have been a couple of greedy middlemen involved if Brondby's claim was also true. Anyway, I now knew that it was a game about money, and you have to play it cool. It felt great to exploit the press for once and with a little manipulation get the director into a dialogue so quickly.

In the days that followed Brondby presented me with some pretty good offers. I remember once we were going to play in Aalborg, and as we stood in the airport there was a magnificent big BMW on display. I stood there, admiring the motor, when Bjerregaard came up to me.

'You could have one of those, no problem!' he said.

A few days later, he called me to set up a meeting. I turned up with my solicitor, Jan Gronlund, having realised that some sort of legal back-up was imperative. We talked about a lot of different things. Gronlund was incredibly hard-hitting, and later on Bjerregaard asked me, mainly in jest, not to bring him along to future meetings.

Things gradually fell into place. Agreement was reached on my price, and I was given the go-ahead by Per Bjerregaard: 'Negotiate a deal!' On 9 June I went to Manchester and had my first big meeting with the United management. We didn't quite finalise the contract that day, but I returned home to

Denmark the day after in the knowledge that my next club was almost certain to be Manchester United.

Not long after that we reached final agreement, and my childhood dream had come true. I was on my way to Old Trafford.

5 Theatre of Dreams

'After hearing the result, I dashed out into the street, and at that moment I saw Steve Bruce, my neighbour and United's captain, come rushing out of his front door. After about ten minutes the first cars started to arrive, and about an hour later the whole squad was gathered at Steve Bruce's house. As you can imagine, it developed into a tremendous party; 50 bottles of champagne, 30 bottles of wine, several hundred beers and an unspecified number of bottles of spirits were consumed. The party lasted until the next morning, even though Alex Ferguson naturally rang to remind us that we had a game the next day.'

S O THERE I WAS in the summer of 1991 at the age of 27 at Manchester United's training ground at Salford, The Cliff, for the very first time. And sitting there with me was Mark Hughes – a legend in my eyes. And Bryan Robson. They were now my new team-mates, and I was a little bit shy to say the least. I was also slightly embarrassed to discover that there were a number of players whose names I didn't even know. I experienced that acute sense of self-awareness you feel when you find yourself in a completely new environment. But it was immensely exciting.

After sixteen months of training under Morten Olsen I was physically in top form, and this surprised my team-mates a bit because they had apparently never seen a goalkeeper who was able to run. And certainly not one who could actually play football. The goalkeepers were usually left on one side and allowed to stand there kicking half-volleys to each other, while the others played in squares, or 'five against two' as it's called. I protested about this arrangement straight away, and it was changed immediately.

A couple of days before that first training session I had been met at the airport by Norman Davies, Manchester United's kit assistant, who picked me up together with my ten sports bags full of clothes – I wasn't sure how long I would have to provide for myself – and drove me to the Ambelhurst Hotel. This hotel was quickly given the nickname 'Fawlty Towers' by all the friends and associates who either had dinner with us there or stayed there while they were in

Manchester. The hotel is a bit of a Manchester United watering-hole where players often go to eat lunch or have a glass of beer after games, in spite of the fact that the owner, Michael Prophet, is a fanatical Manchester City fan. United often held victory celebrations there – and there were quite a number of those.

This was where I was going to stay, for the time being. The Ambelhurst is not a particularly big hotel, but you can't call it small either. There are about 40 rooms and it offers an excellent standard of personal service which is based on Proph's incredibly wide range of contacts who have, in my experience, never failed to meet the needs of the hotel's guests. Bente and the children really enjoyed staying there. So even though the hotel did not perhaps look particularly appealing at first sight, it proved to be the most comfortable way imaginable of adapting ourselves to the English way of life. It is sheltered, but accessible, a good way outside the centre of Manchester, with plenty of social activities and a children's playground; Danish guests who over the years have visited us have developed their own personal attachment to the place. They made their own reservations for the hotel from Denmark, without contacting Bente or me – which gives you some idea of how accommodating the hotel is. We never had any cause for regrets, and the Ambelhurst played a very positive role in our life in England.

But the first few months in England were not without problems. When I first arrived, I did not have a proper contract with the club. I had drawn up a framework agreement with the chairman, Martin Edwards, which had been sealed with a handshake – a mutual understanding based on the good intentions which both parties shared.

However, at that time Manchester United were in the throes of reorganising their set-up so as to become a fully-fledged plc, listed on the Stock Exchange. Until this operation was completed there was no possibility of signing a full contract. I wouldn't say this made me nervous, but all the same I had a feeling that I was serving a kind of probationary period while I ran around working hard at The Cliff.

The club went to Norway for its pre-season tour, and it was there that I played my first games for United. Everything went much better than I had expected, and I think my performances convinced my team-mates that I wasn't just any old keeper who had been bought cheaply from one of the minor footballing countries, but that I was a man they could rely on, with whom they could build a future.

On the day we arrived home from Norway, we had to fly to Aberdeen to play yet another practice match. That was on 6 August 1991, and the deadline for a new player to be eligible for European competition was 8 August. We would still be in Aberdeen on that date, so if I was going to be permitted to be available for selection for the UEFA Cup, I had to sign that contract immediately. I was called to Martin Edwards's office to discuss what should have been a formality, but a number of minor problems had arisen in relation to our agreement and we had to sit down and discuss things once again.

No blood was drawn, but I experienced for the first time – and certainly not the last – just how tough a negotiator Edwards can be. My agent, Rune Hauge, and I were just as stubborn as Edwards, though. I had been at the peak of my form in Norway and had already shown them that I was the right man for the job, so we stuck to our guns, and in the end we got what we were entitled to, according to what we had agreed several months before. There was nothing really dramatic about it, but it took a lot of time to iron out every last little detail, and it meant that I came very near to missing the plane to Aberdeen. But finally the contract was signed, and I was a happy man. Now I was 100 per cent under contract as a Manchester United player for a period of four years, which must have inspired me. In Aberdeen I was voted Man of the Match for the first time in my new career, and I have still got the five-litre bottle of whisky that accompanied the honour. I think about three fingers of it have been drunk.

Eventually the new season got under way, and I made my debut at Old Trafford on 17 August 1991 against Notts County. The crowd of 46,278 gave me that goosepimple-inducing sensation of collective power for the first time in my life, and we had no difficulty in using this support to secure a 2–0 victory over our visitors. Hughes and Robson scored, one in each half, and I was thoroughly convinced that I had made the right decision about coming to Manchester. There was such obvious talent in that team, together with the necessary experience, that already after my first game I started to dream about the rapid fulfilment of my avowed ambition: to win the English League.

In order to gain a real sense of that team's potential, you only have to look again at the line-up for my first appearance. Another reason for doing so is that it brings back such fond memories for me. The team was as follows: Schmeichel, Irwin, Blackmore, Bruce, Ferguson, Parker, Robson, Ince, McClair, Hughes and Kanchelskis. Pallister was brought on instead of Ince, and Giggs replaced Ferguson. That was simply a dream team, and we were flying from the word go. Even at that early stage in the squad's development (apart from me, only Denis Irwin and Ryan Giggs would feature in the Treble-winning squad of 1999) we had a sense of being invincible, and we played thirteen games before we suffered a defeat, when Sheffield Wednesday beat us 3–2 at Hillsborough towards the end of October.

We didn't lose a game after that for the rest of 1991, and only Leeds were able to keep up with us. But we started 1992 in a rather depressing way. On New Year's Day we were overwhelmed by Queens Park Rangers, losing 1–4 at Old Trafford. I won't go into that game in any detail, but after that things went well for us again, and we kept our place until the last week of the season, when we were cut down to size by a packed programme, with five games in a fortnight. First we drew 1–1 at Luton, then we lost 2–1 at home to Nottingham Forest. This was followed two days later by a 1–0 defeat at Upton Park, and then we lost 2–0 at Anfield on the same day that Leeds won the championship by beating Sheffield United 3–2 in a match in which Sheffield conceded two crazy goals. We wrapped up the season by beating Spurs 3–1 at Old Trafford on 2 May, but by then it was academic.

Naturally it was deeply frustrating to lose out like that at the death, but we paid the price for a hectic run-in. At least we were able to celebrate the fact that we had won the European Super Cup and the League Cup, beating Nottingham Forest 1–0 in April. And, from a personal point of view, I had a brilliant summer when I helped Denmark win the European Championship, which naturally ranks as one of my greatest triumphs.

The 1992/93 season turned out to be an historic one for the club, which won its first championship since 1967, and in the process became the first ever Premier League champions. But the season didn't get off to a very good start. We lost our first two games, drew the third, and had a real goalscoring problem which wasn't solved until Eric Cantona joined United that November. After that our luck turned, and we went ten games in a row without defeat. The path to the championship was laid, and when things went down the drain for our closest rivals, Aston Villa, there was no stopping us.

In Denmark we have an expression 'to achieve something while you're sleeping', which means that you gain something without making any effort of your own. This happens very seldom, but I literally won my first championship medal while I was asleep.

As things turned out, Aston Villa had to play Oldham on the Sunday, a game they couldn't afford to lose because it would mean United would become champions. Our game against Blackburn Rovers wasn't until the day after, and I had therefore been to training that Sunday and taken a nap afterwards, as I usually do. When I woke up an hour later, I tuned in to Teletext to see the result of the Aston Villa game. There were still five minutes to go, but Oldham were winning 1–0. Those were five long minutes for me! I switched off the TV, turned on the radio, turned the radio off again, played for a while on the piano, turned on the TV again, went back to the radio, and finally I lay down on the floor behind the sofa with my head buried in my arms. And then the final whistle blew. Oldham had won, and we had become champions of England! After 26 long years, Manchester United were League champions again, and I was a member of the team that had done it!

After hearing the result, I dashed out into the street, and at that moment I saw Steve Bruce, my neighbour and United's captain, come rushing out of his front door. After about ten minutes the first cars started to arrive, and about an hour later the whole squad was gathered at Steve Bruce's house. As you can imagine, it developed into a tremendous party; 50 bottles of champagne, 30 bottles of wine, several hundred beers and an unspecified number of bottles of spirits were consumed. The party lasted until the next morning, even though Alex Ferguson naturally rang to remind us that we had a game the next day.

There was a fantastic atmosphere when we arrived at Old Trafford around midday – some of us bleary-eyed – to prepare ourselves for the game against Blackburn. There was no end to the jubilation among our supporters. Ferguson brought us back down to earth: 'We are the champions now; go out and prove it!' It goes without saying that we took the game seriously. Anything less would have been unfair to the 40,400 spectators who had come to cheer us. To mark the occasion, fans were permitted to take flags with them into Old Trafford, and it seemed to me as if everyone had made use of the opportunity. That occasion still lives in my memory as one of the games where the atmosphere at the ground was genuinely special.

And the game lived up to the occasion, even though Kevin Gallacher put Blackburn ahead in the eighth minute. From that moment onwards we put the effects of the previous night's party behind us and played probably our best game of the season, while the whole of Old Trafford swung to and fro in perfect time. We scored some incredibly good goals, starting with Ryan Giggs, who screwed a free kick into the net from fully 30 yards. Paul Ince put us ahead after Cantona had paved the way, and in the last minute Gary Pallister scored direct from another free kick for his only goal of the season. Blackburn must have felt slightly humiliated.

For the United players, this was a wonderful time. The Ambelhurst Hotel was the venue for a gigantic celebration involving players, management and our families. The next day we all went to Chester racecourse, where we were seated outdoors in the middle circle of the course and spent the day eating seafood and drinking champagne. We relaxed, enjoyed the wonderful sunshine and – I must admit – the only horse I remember seeing that day was a police horse!

The celebrations lasted all that week, and it wasn't just the players enjoying themselves: Manchester United's enormous number of fans were cock-a-hoop. But everyone was conscious of the fact that we still had one game left to play, the following Sunday at Selhurst Park against Wimbledon, and an appetite still existed among fans and players alike for more football, more victories.

When Sunday arrived, Selhurst Park was simply invaded by United fans, who probably accounted for 25,000 of the 30,000 crowd at the ground. No one wanted to miss that golden moment when the trophy finally came into our possession, and I mean that quite literally because our fans poured on to the pitch when we were about to do a lap of honour and prevented our victory procession. There was no sign of trouble or any other irregularity, it was just a question of uncontrollable joy spilling over, and we were happy to share the triumph. I made sure I got hold of the match ball and dashed into the changing room with it. To this very day that ball is on display in the United museum.

For me it was a glorious season. I had played in every game, and in 22 of them I had managed not to let in a goal. This earned me the nickname 'Mr Clean Sheet', and I made no attempt to prevent anyone from using it.

Winning the championship led to serious considerations for the club's management. It was felt that long-term plans should now be made. It was obvious that Manchester United had a high class team which in terms of age provided security for the future. For that reason the club decided to draw up long-term contracts with the players. I, too, began negoti-ations concerning the extension of my contract and they turned out to be long and tough. I have always followed some fairly simple principles when it comes to financial matters: I consider them carefully when I'm negotiating, then I make a stand. Apart from that I don't think very much about them. But I have always held the opinion that I should get what I was worth, and that point of view was underlined in the demands I put to the club. And I kept to them.

Unfortunately, I felt that the negotiations were rather exhausting. In many ways they took too much focus away from what interested me most of all: playing good football. It took almost a year before the contract was signed. This was an unnecessary inconvenience because when it came down to it I was granted all the demands I had made. It was also rather unpleasant that the general public, through the media, virtually took part in the negotiations. Paul Ince and I were referred to as 'the contract rebels', a tag which had no basis in fact and which was also an unwarranted interference in my private affairs. As in so many other cases, those journalists who made such a fuss about all this had no real insight into the situation they were so pleased to write about.

Of course, we also played a lot of football while all this was going on. As Premier League champions we had our title to defend, and all the other clubs wanted so badly to claim our scalps, an eagerness that was apparent in a number of games. All the same we got off to a flying start, losing just one of our first 25 games – against Chelsea at Stamford Bridge – in the process establishing a comfortable lead of thirteen points over Blackburn Rovers, who at that time were the club breathing down our necks. The only disappointment we suffered was when the Turkish club Galatasaray prevented us from progressing in the Champions' League. This top European competition had now become a natural hunting-ground for us, and we felt quite certain that given time we could make our mark on this struggle between the elite European clubs.

It was during the 1993/94 season, in the game against Blackburn on Boxing Day, that I succeeded in introducing English fans to one of my specialities: my active participation in corners. Even though we had put Blackburn under a lot of pressure, we were undoubtedly in trouble. There were two minutes left to play, and we were trailing 1–0 due to a goal scored by that man Kevin Gallacher. Then we were awarded a corner, and I used the opportunity to dash up the pitch with intent to cause confusion. I succeeded. The crowd was confused, our bench was confused – Ferguson watched my display shaking his head – and so were Blackburn's defenders, who allowed Paul Ince enough room to crack the ball into the net after Tim Flowers had only managed to parry the first attempt. I didn't hear a single bad word about my unorthodox behaviour after the game. And the two points we saved as a result played a crucial role towards the end of the season, when things really started to get a bit tight in April.

By Easter Blackburn had fought their way back up and were just three points behind us. Fortunately for us, a bit of breathing space was created when Wimbledon flogged them 4–1, while we took three points with a 1–0 win over Liverpool. Shortly after that things went wrong again when Blackburn beat us 2–0, which meant that we were back in the same situation, but come 2 May United had safely retained the Premier League title, and once again we had a comfortable cushion and could celebrate our triumph without having to play for it as Blackburn lost 2–1 to Coventry. Our meeting with Southampton after that was a pure exhibition match in front of our fans at Old Trafford. We won confidently and convincingly, scoring two goals without reply, and the scenes of jubilation from the previous year were repeated with great pomp and euphoria.

The season was also good from a statistical point of view. Manchester United became only the fourth club in the history of the Football League to win back-to-back championships twice, Liverpool, Aston Villa and Sheffield Wednesday being the other clubs. And on a more personal level, I managed to beat Alex Stepney's record of 76 consecutive League appearances. We also finished off the season nicely by winning the FA Cup 4–0 at the expense of Chelsea, who were the only team we had lost to twice in the League that season.

The following season, 1994/95, turned out to be problematic, both for me and the club. I experienced my first prolonged spell of injury, and I was quite worried about it. The first indication that something was wrong came in September during a game against Liverpool. While I was warming up I suddenly experienced a sensation I'd never had before. It was as if my spinal column had split into two pieces. It was agreed that I should go ahead and play in the game, and then go for an examination afterwards. I took some pills, went out and turned in a really good performance, the highlight of which was a save from a full volley struck from just three yards out in the first minute. We won the game 2–0, but afterwards I was in real agony. My back was stiff and impossible to move, and I had to take a break while I subjected myself to different forms of treatment.

The treatment helped. I was able to play against Crystal Palace at Old Trafford in November, but only for a short while. After one of my first pieces of action the injury reasserted itself, and as I walked off through the tunnel my back once again became increasingly stiff. I had trouble moving, and Bente and I agreed that the best thing to do was to drive home. There was no point in me staying at the ground.

When I got home I lay on the sofa, much against my will, for three whole weeks – shades of my inactivity as a kid in Jutland all those years before. It was a ridiculous and frustrating position for an active man to be in, but there was nothing else for it. I couldn't walk. I couldn't stand up. And we needed all our gallows-humour when I had to go to the toilet. Fortunately, a scan showed that my injury wasn't as serious as I had feared. It turned out to be a slipped disc, and the neurologist explained to me that half the world's population suffers from this affliction without ever being aware of it. I had just been very unlucky. The subsequent treatment – stretching exercises with the aid of various instruments of torture – is not one of my fondest memories. All the same, after seven weeks – the doctor had predicted it would take eight – I was back on my feet again.

I was back on the pitch too, because I was absolutely dying to get back. I missed football. Taking a bit of a risk, I made an appearance against Sheffield United at Bramall Lane in early January on a rain-soaked pitch and on a very windy day. But my back stood up to it, and we won 2–0. Since then I have not been troubled by back injury, but I make sure that I go through a programme of back exercises every single morning.

The season did not bring United any titles, so I won't dig too deep into our list of results. I will only recall that we met West Ham in the final game of the season still with a realistic chance of winning the Premiership, provided that Blackburn lost away to Liverpool and we won at Upton Park. The first condition was fulfilled, but we were simply unable to get the ball to cross the goal-line, despite having all kinds of chances. And the following week we faced Everton in the FA Cup final. Once again we had plenty of chances, while Everton only had one. They scored, we didn't. I suppose runners-up in both the Premier League and the FA Cup wasn't a bad performance, but that provided scant comfort at the time. At the age of 31, I seriously began to think about my future in football.

This tendency grew much stronger as we began to prepare ourselves for the 1995/96 season. We said goodbye to three veterans, all of whom were key players: Paul Ince, Mark Hughes and Andrei Kanchelskis, who left the club for various reasons. To the great surprise of all the players, no new players were bought to replace them. This seemed a bit perturbing in the light of the relatively poor achievements of the previous season. There was talk about the possibility of buying the Dutchman Marc Overmars, but it never got any further than that, and as the start of the new season approached it became clear that Alex Ferguson was planning to fill the empty spaces in the team with a number of young players from the reserves.

The players in question – all of them very well known today – were Gary and Phil Neville, David Beckham, Paul Scholes and Nicky Butt. They turned out to be strong players, but at that time they were inexperienced and, in many people's opinion, they lacked the kind of weight and nous necessary to put Manchester United right back at the top. I shared this concern, which was expressed most clearly – and most memorably – by the former Liverpool defender Alan Hansen on BBC's *Match of the Day*. After the very first game of the season, he said: 'You win nothing with kids.'

Initially it looked as if he was going to be right. We got off to a bad start on 19 August, losing 1–3 against Aston Villa at Villa Park. Perhaps it was a coincidence, perhaps it was nerves; at any rate, after that we really put bite into our game. We won the next five games in a row, and our new young players became almost visibly pumped up with self-confidence. They revelled in a combination of playfulness and a sudden acquisition of maturity which really impressed me. Our tenth game of the season, against Liverpool, saw the welcome return of Eric Cantona after his kung-fu-kick suspension. He scored straight away. He was the creative force behind Nicky Butt's early opener for United, and he equalised with a late penalty.

But in the run-up to Christmas we started to slip. First of all we drew three games, then we lost 0–2 away to Liverpool. On Christmas Eve, Leeds beat us 3–1, and on New Year's Day – in England there isn't much consideration given to footballers with regard to scheduling – we suffered our biggest defeat of the season. Tottenham outclassed us and thrashed us 4–1. In those few weeks we were given a real taste of what a lack of experience can mean.

Alex Ferguson began to be criticised for his decisions, but luckily we managed to turn the tables again. Eric Cantona turned on the power, and the real turning-point for the club was undoubtedly on 4 March when we met our real rivals that season, Newcastle United, away from home. Earlier that season they had built up a twelve-point lead at the top. By March they were four points clear with a game in hand, so that day was by unanimous consent absolutely decisive as to whether or not we could win the Premiership. As so often before, it was Eric Cantona who took matters into his own hands, cutting Newcastle's lead by scoring the only goal of the match.

This defeat really shook Newcastle, and it started our upward surge. When the season finished on 5 May, with the help of an away win over Middlesbrough we were four points ahead of Newcastle. That may sound a lot, but if Newcastle had won and we had lost our final game, they would have been the champions. It was a close-run thing. The special thing about our achievement that year was that we were able to bridge that considerable points gap in the last third of the season. Added to that was the sweet satisfaction of having won the championship again with the help of Alan Hansen's 'kids'. Alex Ferguson had done the right thing after all. Those young players proved that they had what it takes. Paul Scholes scored ten goals in his first season, and David Beckham demonstrated that he was a man to be reckoned with in the future, scoring on seven occasions. In all, we scored no fewer than 73 goals. I let 35 go past me.

The season was also notable because the entire United team supported Liverpool, our arch enemies from Merseyside, for perhaps the first time. This was when Liverpool met Newcastle in a tremendously exciting game at Anfield. Newcastle were one goal up for most of the game – right up to the last few minutes in fact, when Liverpool scored twice. That defeat meant that we moved above Newcastle for the first time that season. So our unique solidarity that day with our traditional rivals proved to be a good investment!

But this episode was soon put behind us as there was one big clash still to be decided that season: the FA Cup final at Wembley. As things had turned out, it was to be a meeting between the two old enemies, Manchester United and Liverpool. Actually, to call these two teams enemies is perhaps a slight understatement; in my experience it is probably more correct simply to refer to the relationship as one of utter hatred. There are many reasons for this. There are deep cultural differences between these two big cities, and Manchester has had more success with its development. In turn, United fans have great difficulty coping with the fact that during the 1970s and 1980s Liverpool were undoubtedly the greatest football team in England, if not Europe. But United now occupy that throne.

So there were great expectations surrounding that year's final, which is always an immense occasion. It is a competition steeped in tradition which is dear to many – just consider the heated nationwide discussions that erupted after Manchester United's announcement that they were withdrawing from the FA Cup in the 1999/2000 season. Traditions are not to be tampered with, and the most traditional part is, of course, the competition's showpiece: the final. Everyone would like to have a ticket for it. For the players it's a very special occasion.

We have our own tradition too: we always stay at Oakley Court by the Thames. This is an old hotel built in a Gothic style, which has made it a natural location for a number of horror films over the years. But when we stay there it's always very pleasant, and the days leading up to the FA Cup final are filled with relaxing pursuits such as boating trips, clay-pigeon shooting and the like. And you can always be certain there will be a television camera nearby, no matter what you're doing. Everything connected with the FA Cup is of interest, but it all takes place in that pleasant and relaxed English manner, where humour is always the dominant ingredient. It's one of the English traits that really appeals to me.

But let's get back to the game in question. It did not turn out to be a particularly exciting one. Eric Cantona crowned his work that season for Manchester United by scoring the only goal of the game, thereby securing for us the Double for the second time, the first English club ever to do so. The first time was in 1994, so we were continuing our impressive run of victories in the 1990s.

This was underlined in the 1996/97 season. We added Ole Gunnar Solskjaer from Norway to the squad, and he didn't hesitate to accept the challenge. He had a great season and finished convincingly as our top scorer with 18 goals in 25 games. It was also Eric Cantona's last season for us. He gave in his notice just after the end of the season and returned to France. But we became champions again. This time our progress was relatively trouble-free: we finished seven points clear of Newcastle, while Arsenal took third place with the same number of points, a warning of the challenge to come in future years from north London.

Once again we played some wonderful football. It was a season in which David Beckham first really showed his true talent with a number of spectacular goals. He scored eight times, each goal more beautiful than the one before. Everyone could see that a megastar had announced his arrival.

The 1997/98 season turned into a slightly disjointed affair for us. We allowed ourselves, for example, to be beaten seven times, twice at home. And with statistics of that kind you do not become English champions. Andy Cole demonstrated his strong scoring abilities and ended as top scorer with fifteen goals. Teddy Sheringham, our new signing from Tottenham, completed his first season by scoring nine goals. And if we are to take a positive view of the season, we did at least finish as runners-up, only one point behind the champions, Arsenal. But disappointment was hanging in the air; that kind of achievement does not really count at this stage of Manchester United's history.

The 1998/99 season, however, was something else – the most successful season in the history of the club, and also my last. I couldn't have finished at a better time.

I am immensely proud to have been a part of this wonderful period in the glorious history of Manchester United. The club will live on, new players and new teams will arrive on the scene, but I know that I have earned myself a sentence or two in one of the most important chapters of all time. That means a lot to me.

6 The Danish National Team

'Peter Schmeichel has had to fight for everything he has achieved. Overseas goalkeepers are seldom given preference when clubs want to make an investment. It's more attractive to buy a goalscorer. That's why I have had to fight to become so good that I couldn't be ignored. It's that mentality that has always given me the strength to make that extra effort, to go that extra mile – absolutely essential if you want to reach the top.'

I CURRENTLY HOLD THE DANISH record for the highest number of international appearances, a figure that improves every time I run out on to the pitch for my country. My career spans twelve years and more than 110 international matches, and includes the finals of the European Championship and the World Cup.

While I was taking stock during the writing of this book, so many memories came flooding back that I knew it was going to be impossible to get everything down. So I decided that I was going to approach my years in the Danish team anecdotally.

I have seen many players come and go and have served under three national team coaches, soon to be four. They have all made an impression on me in their own way but none more so Preben Elkjaer Larsen.

The very first time I met him was while I was playing for Hvidovre. As a celebration of the club's jubilee, Hvidovre's sponsors, the Toms Chocolate Company, arranged a game against Verona, who at that time had Elkjaer in the team. Verona were in the running for the Italian championship that year with Elkjaer playing an all-important role as top scorer. I was one of a small team responsible for the production of the match poster. We had a slight problem because when it went to print we were still not 100 per cent certain that Verona would finish in first place, but we took a chance with it anyway. We had the poster printed billing Verona as Italian champions. Luckily, we got it right.

A couple of days later I was asked to represent Hvidovre at a press conference to which Preben Elkjaer had been invited, so it was something of an occasion. Everyone was behaving like excited kids – 'Preben's coming! Preben's coming!' – and the place was packed with journalists. It was the first press conference I had ever attended, and at that time I hadn't even played for Denmark or done anything else of any note, so of course the press weren't interested in me at all. Preben, who was very late for the press conference, still took the time to say hello to a young, unknown player from Hvidovre. That impressed me a great deal. It is something I have never forgotten.

Unfortunately, just prior to the game Elkjaer managed to pick up an injury. This was rather unfortunate given that many of the spectators who had bought a ticket had done so primarily to see this celebrated footballer in action. Just before the game I ran into him – the two changing rooms were right next door to each other – and cheekily blurted out: 'What's all this then, have you chickened out?'

Elkjaer was no less cheeky with his response. He looked straight at me, and said: 'What are you talking about? Next time we play against each other, I'll bet you £3,000 that I'll score past you!'

He knew perfectly well that I didn't have that kind of money, so he got the better of me on that one. Since then I have met him on many occasions and have grown to like him for his decency, his sense of humour and, not least, his intelligence. Unfortunately, I only managed to play one international game on the same side as him, against West Germany in the European Championship in 1988 when we lost to the host nation 0–2.

But for young lads like me at that time, only on the verge of getting a place on the team that had undoubtedly made its biggest impact during the World Cup finals in Mexico in 1986, both in terms of performances and popularity with the fans, it was a great thrill to be with them. I made my breakthrough in those finals in West Germany and managed to play two games. For John Faxe, Lars Olsen and myself it was a real experience.

I'll never forget one day when we were sitting outside our hotel. Faxe had just been signed by Hamburg SV, and when you are as young as we were, you talk a lot about what you are going to buy with all the money you are going to earn. Faxe announced that he wanted to buy a Mercedes, and over on the other side of the street at that time there was a parked Merc that had caught his fancy. Faxe chatted away, and Preben agreed with him that it was a really good car. Faxe grew increasingly enthusiastic, and confirmed: 'Yes, that's the kind of car I want. Is that what you've got?'

'No,' replied Preben, 'mine's two classes above that one!'

Faxe just sat there gaping!

Later on I met Elkjaer in Italy when I was on a training trip with Brondby. Even though he had no connection with Brondby whatsoever and hardly knew any of the players or the coaching staff, he arrived at our hotel to say hello. Suddenly, he said to the lads, 'By the way, I've got a present for you.' He went out and came back with ten boxes of a good local red wine. He was, and still is, a man of class, and in my opinion he has become a very good football commentator. His powers of analysis are first-rate, and he comes over well on the screen.

The only thing I regret on his behalf is that he was never given enough time to establish the sports channel he attempted to launch recently in Denmark. The concept was right, and if anybody was capable of pulling off the job it was Preben Elkjaer. Unfortunately, the channel was closed down.

But let's get back to the European Championship side of 1988, with whom I made my debut. Prior to that, on 20 May 1987, I had appeared for Denmark's Olympic team in a qualification match away from home against Greece, which we won 5–0. It was something of a revelation for me to play for the 'real' national team, and it became clear that even though the team included quite a number of star players, it was a squad with no prima donnas. I have already spoken of Preben Elkjaer's temperament, and later on I also forged a close relationship with Soren Lerby, even though my introduction to the team was made slightly difficult as a result of certain family entanglements.

For some reason or other, my father-in-law, Svend Aage Hansen, didn't like Soren Lerby. This surprised me somewhat, because Lerby was exactly the kind of player that suited Svend Aage's attitude to the game. But it turned out that he and Lerby's dad, Kaj, had grown up together. Kaj Lerby was a local legend in the Bispebjerg district of Copenhagen, and my father-in-law always said that Soren tried to imitate his father, something that apparently wasn't acceptable. At any rate, I was told time and time again that if there was any trouble with Soren Lerby, I should just put him in his place. It never came to that – Soren never yelled at me. To this day, Soren and I are good friends and we talk often. We see each other whenever our paths cross. He is currently in Monaco.

Another player from the 1988 World Cup team who has come to mean a lot to me and my family is Jesper Olsen. With Olsen and his wife Sarah, along with our mutual friends John and Rachel Mamelok, we have enjoyed a very warm and affectionate close-knit relationship. Bente and I miss them now that we no longer live in England. Fortunately, the world is getting smaller – it doesn't take much to jump on a plane so I'm sure we shall continue to see each other regularly.

I have always been a great fan of that particular Danish team. When they got through to the semi-final against Spain in 1984 in France, I embarked on a nineteen-hour coach trip to Lyons to cheer them on. I was there for two hours, saw the game, and then took the nineteen-hour coach trip back to Denmark. However, my interest in the Danish national team at this point proved to be rather unfortunate for my club, Hvidovre. I arrived home from France in the morning, together with several other players from our team, and that evening we had to play against Brondby in a Carlsberg Grand Prix match. We were slaughtered 7–1. Nothing to be proud of. But for Bjarne Jensen, who was later to become my team-mate, it was a great evening. He scored two goals! That was a feat he had never managed before that day, nor has he ever managed it since, so of course he never fails to mention that particular highlight of his career!

Four years had passed since then and suddenly there I was

in the team together with all the big names of Danish football. Of course my tabloid-fed, rumour-mill notions about how star players behave were turned upside down. Seen from the outside, it's as if they're granted some sort of godlike status, and you have the feeling that you know just what they could be like, but the picture you have can only be wrong. Once you meet them, you can't fail to notice the huge difference between the public image and the reality. And the same thing has obviously happened to me. A lot of people think that they know me. They have at least an impression of what they think I am like on the basis of the images and stories they have seen and heard. But I'm probably not like that at all. We are all ordinary people, it's just that some of us have succeeded in developing our talent for playing football to a higher level.

In West Germany in 1988, it was certainly great fun to be included in the team, but as far as our results were concerned it was a nightmare: three defeats in a row (Spain 2–3, West Germany 0–2, Italy 0–2), and straight back to Copenhagen. It was a case of a team falling apart at the seams.

An era had come to an end, and it was marked by a big blow-out in Nyhavn, by the quay in Copenhagen. Among those present were Jesper Olsen, Michael Laudrup, Soren Lerby, Frank Arnesen and Ivan Nielsen. Lars Olsen, Faxe and myself were at the party too. The evening turned out to be a very positive experience for me. Even though the team was burnt out and had achieved very poor results, a lot of people came forward and expressed their admiration for what the team had achieved overall. That was very pleasing to hear.

This attitude stems from the fact that there is a great deal of defiance in the Danish national character. We don't really like anyone to tell us how to do anything. Being defiant is often portrayed in a negative light, but when defiance is used to combat a power which sees itself as naturally superior, it becomes a very potent instrument. It took the team many years to get to the stage where we could be defiant on the pitch and not end up with egg on our faces, and there is no doubt that Sepp Piontek had a great deal of influence on the development that has taken place. It's a healthy state to be in: Denmark, even though it's a very small country, has produced a number of extremely good results in international football. Of that there can be no doubt.

No one really had any great expectations of German coach Sepp Piontek when he was appointed in 1979, and it took nearly four years for him to establish himself and begin to achieve good results. But he used those four years in a very creative way, asking himself the question: 'Why has this country, which has produced so many good players, never won anything?' In this way he made a contribution to laying the foundations for the growth of professional football in Denmark. He also ensured that professional Danish players abroad were expected to come home and play for the national team.

In my opinion he certainly chose the right path in his quest for success, because a kind of natural creativity exists in Denmark which is nurtured by our liberal upbringing together with imaginative teaching in kindergartens and schools. It is precisely this quality that Piontek tapped into and exploited on the football pitch. It is often creativity that wins football matches. And it was a good thing that this new way of looking at the possibilities inherent in Danish football came from the outside. It has to be remembered that professional football in Denmark did not exist until 1978. All coaches and players were essentially amateurs, and this obviously severely limited the potential for insight and development.

Actually, Piontek was not particularly experienced when he arrived on the scene. But he was a clever man who had great vision, believed in what he said, and had a wonderful ability to charm the press to such an extent that they were often like putty in his hands.

Nevertheless, it is debatable whether or not Sepp possessed the right kind of insight in terms of when players should be brought in to and left out of his regular squad. It is possible to argue that he could have carried out his generational changes between 1986 and 1988 in a smoother fashion, but it very much came down to a question of taste and judgement, whether or not the man at the helm was prepared to take a gamble in the final rounds of a competition or choose to rely on a team of regulars. At any rate, it was the right thing to do to say goodbye to Elkjaer, Lerby, Arnesen and all the other great heroes after the European Championship in 1988. Michael Laudrup stayed with us, but it was a new-look team. Now it was up to people like me to assume responsibility after having played just a few games under the old set-up – and at that time the qualifying games for the 1990 World Cup were looming.

Unfortunately, we didn't qualify. It proved impossible to establish enough of a routine, even though the team had considerable potential. In the first game against Greece in Athens we wasted two or three good scoring chances and had to settle for a 1–1 draw. In the next game, against Bulgaria at home, we were leading 1–0 and were looking fairly secure when the Bulgarians were awarded a free kick around the halfway line. Kent Nielsen was summoned by the referee and was given a warning. The Bulgarians took the free kick quickly, Nielsen hadn't managed to get back in time, and the Bulgarians exploited the gap in the defence to equalise.

We had dropped four points in the first two games, but we went on to play some wonderful football. Romania were sent home from The Park in Copenhagen on the wrong end of a 3–0 scoreline, we beat Bulgaria 2–0 away from home, and in a legendary and entertaining return game at The Park on a beautiful day in May we crushed Greece 7–1. It was such a consummate team effort that there were seven different names on the Danish scoresheet.

But after that, everything fell apart. In the last game on a dismal November day in 1989, we faced eleven Romanians about whom Soren Lerby later remarked: 'They certainly hadn't drunk buttermilk before the game!' We got off to a good start with an early goal from Flemming Poulsen, but we were terribly nervous. The game's result would decide whether we made it to Italy or not, and Sepp Piontek had decided to bring Lerby back into the team instead of Jan Heintze, who Sepp thought might have trouble in the air. This meant that the defence was reshuffled. Kent Nielsen was put at left-back, a position he had never played in before.

Obviously, this created a certain amount of uneasiness, and – looking back – was a clear tactical error. But I wouldn't blame the defeat on that. The Romanians were unbelievably aggressive and put us under pressure all the way through the game. We were unable to find a way to counteract their style and succumbed to a 3–1 defeat. It was a bitterly disappointing moment. We hadn't played that badly, and perhaps the result wasn't that surprising, but we knew we should have done better in previous games against Bulgaria and Greece. The result was a real shock to the system because just one month earlier we have comfortably beaten a pretty ineffective Romanian side on home turf. Clearly, home advantage made a big difference over the two games.

Then came a change of manager. Sepp Piontek had done his job, now it was up to Richard Moller Nielsen to make sure that we qualified for the European Championship in Sweden in 1992. We didn't make it through those qualifying stages either, but we made it to Sweden all the same!

Our great triumph there is described in the next chapter, so I'm going to wind things forward a year or so and write about one of the most disappointing matches I've ever played in. It took place in Seville on 18 November 1993, and it was a decisive match for us in terms of our qualification for the World Cup in 1994. At nine o'clock in the evening, as is the tradition in Spain, the referee blew his whistle for the start of the match. Just a few minutes later, Michael Laudrup intercepted a mishit goal kick by the Spanish goalkeeper Zubizaretta. Michael was one to one with the goalkeeper, and the Spaniard was forced to pull the emergency brake just outside the penalty area. Zubizaretta was promptly given his marching orders, and Spain were forced to play almost the whole game with ten men.

In spite of this, things went wrong for us. The Spanish reserve goalkeeper played the game of his life and the match turned into something of a personal nightmare for me. It was my thirtieth birthday, and we had Spain under pressure when they were awarded a corner on the right. It all looked fairly harmless, and I judged it to be my ball. As I moved out of my goal to reach the ball, I was obstructed by Bakero, which allowed Hierro to head softly into the goal unchallenged. I was, and still am, completely convinced that I was fouled, but the referee thought otherwise. Plenty of people took the view that my bungled interception gave Spain their victory, allowing them to qualify. I'm not afraid to assume the responsibility, but I believe I should have been given a free kick. On the other hand, if I had stayed in my goal it would have been easy for Kim Vilfort to head the ball away, but he was convinced that it was my ball. It wasn't exactly the way I had expected to celebrate my thirtieth birthday, and it definitely qualifies as one of the worst days of my life. The most bitter pill to swallow was the fact that we had conceded only two goals in the space of twelve qualifying games. Spain scored one, Ireland the other, and both goals cost us our place on that plane to the United States. In such situations, though, you have to tell yourself that it's only football and that life goes on. I have enjoyed so many hugely positive experiences in the game that that particular night in Seville is nothing but a minor detail in my memory bank.

The experience made us doubly determined to qualify for the World Cup in France in 1998, under the guidance of our new manager, Bo Johansson. We were doubly happy to finally achieve qualification and I have written about the 1998 competition in chapter 14.

In professional football, a great deal of time is spent travelling and sitting around between games. For many years the Danish national team has had a card playing club. Like all other football clubs I know of, we play cards in airports, on buses, in hotel rooms and wherever else we can. But now that I am the only one left of the old team, the club has been reduced to me sitting in my room playing solitaire! I guess this was inevitable when you play for a team for several years with people your own age who gradually drop out one by one.

The last time the card club was in action was during France 98. We played every night from nine to eleven at night. We called the game poker, but I seriously doubt that many professional poker players would have recognised our version of the game. We had enormous fun and it was a great way of killing time.

In major tournaments like the World Cup, which can last up to a month, it is very easy to get seriously bored. Incarcerated in the training camp, you quickly begin to feel that you are going crazy. That's not conducive to performance or team spirit. The card club played such an important role in this respect. We played for money and on occasion I would lose heavily, but in the next game I would win the money back just as fast. I don't believe you can play anything properly if there's nothing at stake. By playing for money we kept proceedings on a serious level instead of just fooling around.

Much has been written in the Danish press about gambling in the national team, but gambling isn't how I would define what was going on. One story claimed that during one game £9,000 was supposedly won and lost. As you can imagine, this made for sensational headlines and much finger-wagging, but I have never participated in a game in which that kind of money changed hands. Either it was before my time or on an evening when I didn't play. No one has ever lost more than they could afford, and no one has ever become rich as a result of one of our card games. The card club has a wonderfully nice atmosphere. I miss it a great deal!

7 European Glory

'We are no longer a "nearly" nation which year after year stumbles at the finishing line. We made it to the top, and gave football-loving Danes everywhere a new and welcome identity. No one can take that away from us, and for me the roar of the jubilant crowd at the Nya Ullevi Stadium in Gothenburg on 26 June 1992 is one of the greatest experiences of my footballing career.'

I N DENMARK THERE IS A CONSTANT, and rather pointless, debate about which Danish national team was the best of all time. Was it the so-called 'champagne team' that blitzed its way through the 1986 World Cup in Mexico, until Spain put a big fat spoke in the wheel? Or was it the 1992 European Championship side that went all the way in Sweden? Or was it perhaps the World Cup team that wiped out Nigeria and played on a par with Brazil in the World Cup in France in 1998? The discussion can go on for ever, but for me there is no doubt about it: winning the European Championship in Sweden was the greatest Danish footballing achievement of all time.

There's no getting away from it: in football, it's results that count. Because the 1992 triumph was achieved by a team that played outstanding football, a team that got mentally stronger as the championship progressed, I know that our victory in Sweden was no fluke. The best team won, even if fortune favoured us – not least of all in the final against Germany. Even so, you have to create your own luck. You have to earn it. It was a by-product of the immense effort our team made, in the face of a plague of injuries.

The Danish team that year certainly wasn't labouring under any great expectations. We only made it into the final rounds because Yugoslavia were prevented from taking part for political reasons. Instead of going on our holidays we were suddenly given the opportunity to take part, and we gladly took it. I have grown tired of the myth that Denmark sent a summer-holiday team to Sweden. On the contrary, we were all very fit. Our domestic club competitions had just finished, and a week before the first game in Sweden we had played against CIS (the Commonwealth of Independent States) in a thrilling and very even game. So the team that met Graham Taylor's England on 11 June in Malmo for its first appearance in the championship was both physically strong and highly motivated. It turned out to be an encouraging start for us. It ended in a goalless draw, but we came closest to scoring when John Faxe hit the post. In any case, the game clearly demonstrated that we were not the late-entry lame ducks of the competition, and we were highly optimistic when we met Sweden in Stockholm three days later.

That turned out to be a magnificent match, and we didn't deserve to lose 0–1. As the game progressed, we grew stronger and stronger, but despite pressing hard we just couldn't manage an equaliser. We felt totally spent, and deeply, deeply disappointed. It was like a morgue in the dressing room after the game; we were convinced that we were going out of the competition. So did Jorn Mader from TV2; he ended his report by saying that was that for Denmark in the tournament. Luckily, neither he nor we were right.

In the last game of the first round we had to play France, who had looked very strong in their first two matches. Our hopes for a win were limited, but I thought a victory was a possibility. And it turned out to be a wonderful evening for us in Malmo. While we were standing in the players' tunnel, just before we went on to the pitch, some of the French players began to brag to John Sivebaek. They knew him from French club football, and they let Sivebaek know in no uncertain terms that it was going to be France's game. 'So just take it easy, boys,' they said, 'and don't spoil anything for us!' That provocation spread like wildfire down our line, and I'm quite certain that it played a part in firing up our team. At any rate, we played excellent, entertaining football against a French side that had been installed as tournament favourites. Henrik Larsen opened the scoring, then Jean-Pierre Papin equalised with a crisp shot into the left-hand side of the goal, but Lars Elstrup extinguished all hope for the French with a goal from close range. Suddenly the Danish 'holiday team' was actually in the semi-finals. This was a great surprise, not least for the press, and the Danish contingent almost doubled in size within the space of a few days.

At this time a number of things happened which I think had a decisive influence on the rest of the competition. The more attention we received, the calmer the atmosphere surrounding our team became. The Danish manager, Richard Moller Nielsen, made it his policy to absorb any distractions and deal with any problems or enquiries himself, so that his players could go about their day-to-day business in a particularly relaxed environment. He did a good job, because they were completely carefree days. We enjoyed the experience instead of being tense and afraid.

So it was in a balanced frame of mind that we ran on to the field in Gothenburg on 22 June to face Holland in a game which has justifiably gone down in Danish sporting history. It was not just the fact that we won; the game contained all the elements you could hope to find in a classic drama. It was a brilliant match. We were in the lead twice thanks to two goals by Henrik Larsen, and both times the Dutch managed to hit back. There was excitement and drama aplenty before we could bow out as winners after the penalty shoot-out. During regulation time, extra time and the shoot-out there was so little difference between the two teams that both sides deserved to go on to the final. But we had the necessary luck, best illustrated by our final penalty. Kim Christofte stepped up to take it. He started playing some kind of mind-game with the Dutch goalkeeper, Hans van Breuklin. Christofte's intention was to disturb the Dutchman's concentration. He succeeded, and proceeded to stroke the ball in rather arrogantly. All of Denmark roared.

Our euphoria was dampened by Henrik Andersen's ugly accident which turned out to be much more serious than we anticipated. At first I thought he had simply twisted his knee and, at worst, strained his ligaments. But it turned out he had fractured his knee-cap. For a footballer, there are few injuries worse than that. Sivebaek and Lars Olsen were injured too, with a pulled thigh muscle and a back injury respectively, but Andersen's misfortune put these into context.

We were utterly exhausted. In the triumph of victory, we managed to put the injuries to the back of our minds. We were in the final.

Germany, our opponents, were naturally the favourites before the game. Their squad had wide experience of playing big matches in the latter stages of a competition. But we weren't worried at all about being the underdogs. It suited our strategy perfectly, and our ever-increasing self-confidence was high, without developing into over-confidence. It was a comfort to us that the venue for the final, the Nya Ullevi Stadium in Gothenburg, gave us the small advantage of playing close to home. The red and white Danish flag, the Dannebrog, clearly dominated in the crowd.

To this day I have difficulty understanding how we actually got through that game. I don't think I will ever understand what really happened. As I mentioned, Sivebaek had strained a muscle and other members of the team were clearly affected by the four games we had played within two weeks, but the team rose magnificently to the occasion, driven by a zest for success and an incredibly high standard of workmanship on that glorious day.

I had the kind of luck Denmark needed early on in the game when Jurgen Klinsmann broke through on the right side of the penalty area. He shot hard and flat to my left and I just managed to get the very tips of my fingers on to the ball and glance it past the post. I consider that to be one of the best saves of my career; it was certainly of vital importance, because I still have the feeling that things would have gone wrong for us if the Germans had taken the lead at that stage.

When John Faxe Jensen put us into the lead with a cracking shot, following heroic work by Flemming Poulsen, a buzz of incredulity began to work its way around the stadium. The goal gave us extra strength, which we needed to cope with the pressure the Germans subsequently put us under. In the second half it took a number of small miracles to prevent the Germans from equalising. Kent Nielsen made the kind of goal-line clearance that only comes off perhaps once in a hundred times, and I myself was fortunate with a couple of interceptions, one of which – a one-handed scoop that

Playing for Gladsaxe-Hero, 1983

With my son Kasper, only four days old

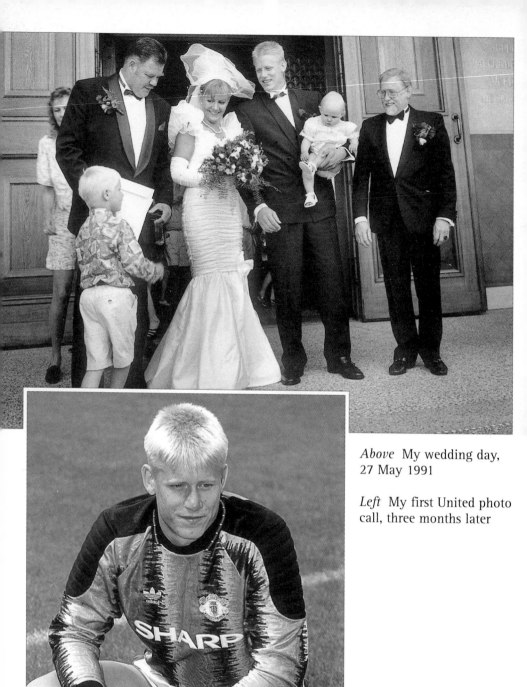

Above My wedding day,
27 May 1991

Left My first United photo
call, three months later

When I first arrived at Old Trafford, Bryan Robson, Mark Hughes and Steve Bruce were the spine of the team. All three players were totally committed to the cause and, in their own way, hugely influential. Robson and Bruce are now managers and 'Sparky' may well be heading that way too.

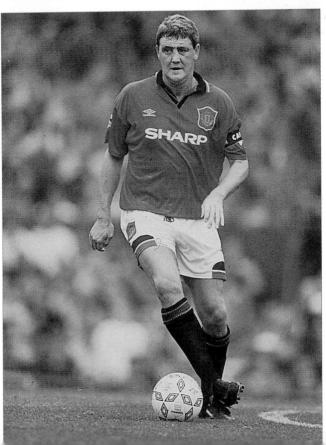

Left Saving a Dutch penalty at Euro 92

Right Scoring my one and only United goal, against Rotor Volgograd in the UEFA Cup, September 1995

Below left Lifting the 1994 Premier League trophy

Below right Celebrating at Wembley after winning the FA Cup in 1996

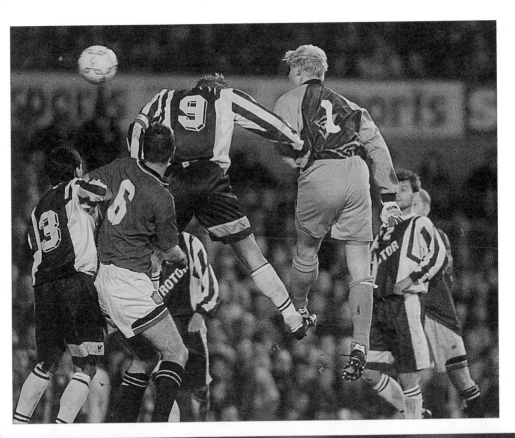

Above May 1997 – Eric Cantona proudly shows off the Premier League trophy

Right Cantona had style, grace, poise, strength and a sharp football brain

Peter Schmeichel, pig farmer.
A memorable Reebok
commercial

Left Playing for my country always gives me a huge thrill

Below Sir Alex Ferguson – the trophy says it all

plucked the ball out of the air – became something of a classic. The manner of that save wasn't an expression of any kind of over-confidence; I simply couldn't get both arms up to the ball, and I was therefore forced to make do with one hand.

As the match progressed and we continued to shut out the opposition, the Germans grew more and more demoralised. When Kim Vilfort increased our lead towards the end of the game, things just fell apart for them. They realised it was Denmark's day, and that they had no chance whatsoever of stopping us. Later, Lars Olsen lifted the trophy towards the dark evening sky and the Danish fans went mad. It was final proof of the fact that everything had come together for the team during the competition, but I still felt bemused as to how and why it had all worked out in our favour.

After the final we were informed that we could either fly straight back to Denmark overnight or stay in Gothenburg and celebrate. It wasn't difficult to choose, and we partied all through the night on the quay at the marina where we were staying. It was very late – I should say very early – when we got to bed, and most of us didn't sleep for much more than an hour and a half.

There was a definite air of exhilaration on the coach the next morning as we prepared to leave for the airport. We couldn't set off straight away because Kim Christofte was missing. This wasn't really a surprise for any of us since he's a bit of an independent spirit and often goes his own way. They checked to see if he was sitting down on a nearby stone, which had become known as 'Christofte's Stone' because he often sat there thinking or taking pictures of sailing ships, which was one of his great passions. But he was nowhere to be found. In the end Richard Moller Nielsen gave orders for the coach to leave.

When we reached the airport we were driven straight out to the plane – we were, after all, European champions – and just as we were about to board the plane, another coach arrived. The only passenger on it was Christofte. We knew him as a private, very discreet man who always kept well away from the press, but the vision we saw was anything but discreet: he was wearing a straw hat and a very large pair of sunglasses, and in his arms was an enormous teddy bear, a football and, naturally, his indispensable camera. He looked like a typical Danish tourist, and he played that role to perfection for the rest of the day.

There wasn't a dry eye among us when this normally subdued man continued to play the fool on the balcony of the Copenhagen Town Hall in front of several hundred thousand people, whose disbelieving eyes were focused entirely on him! The rest of us were also mucking about: the entire Danish national team, together with the team staff, bounced up and down on the balcony singing: 'Deutschland, Deutschland, alles ist vorbei!' (Germany, Germany, it's all over!). It was really great fun, although I became a little nervous when I suddenly noticed a sign on the entrance to the balcony that read: MAXIMUM EIGHT PEOPLE. I didn't really relax until we were back inside the town hall again, where the Chief Burgomaster of Copenhagen, Kramer Mikkelsen, regrettably proclaimed that our victory in the European Championship was a great day for Copenhagen. I thought that was a bit of a liberty, I must say, but there is no doubt about the fact that Copenhagen gave us a magnificent welcome.

We'd flown back to Denmark on board a Swedish plane, and champagne was served throughout the flight, so we weren't entirely of sound mind when we arrived in Copenhagen. Just before we were about to touch down, the plane rose into the air again and the captain announced that we were going to fly over Copenhagen Town Hall square. Faxe was the first one to realise what was actually going to happen. We'd only been told that there was to be some sort of reception; suddenly, from the air we caught sight of a surging crowd of red and white below us. That was the moment when we realised it wasn't going to be an ordinary day.

At the airport they had lined up all the city's fire engines, and at a guess I would say there were about 5,000 people there to welcome us. After a short wait we were collected by an open bus, and then we were taken on one of the slowest bus rides I have ever experienced. There were people everywhere who wanted to congratulate us, and it was almost impossible to drive through the crowds. At one point along the route the bus came to a complete halt, but we used the opportunity to get hold of some liquid refreshment before the ride continued. The only real problem was that the bus wasn't equipped with a toilet. I think I must have been in a state of high excitement, because I failed to notice that my team-mates had taken it in turns to jump off the bus in order to avail themselves of the facilities at hairdresser's salons, bars and shops along the route. I just stood there for a full two hours, and was on the point of exploding when we finally arrived at the town hall. It only took me about fifteen seconds to reach the toilet.

My visit to the toilet meant that I missed the first part of the official reception programme, but there was so much more going on that I didn't mind too much. We were European champions, and that was what mattered most of all. It was one of the most memorable days of my life. Every time I cross the square of Copenhagen Town Hall, I jump with delight and the memories come flooding back.

Four years later we had the opportunity to defend our title in England but we didn't progress past the group stage. We got the same results in the first round that we had had in Sweden – a win, a defeat and a draw against Turkey, Croatia and Portugal respectively – but this time we didn't have the same kind of luck, and we were eliminated. It was not a particularly pleasant experience for us as reigning champions, but there were a number of different things that didn't click in England in 1996.

However, I can no more explain what went wrong in England than I can identify why we had such a fantastic run in Sweden. There were a number of practical things that failed to work out properly, and in that respect I must take part of the blame because I was involved in the choice of hotel for the team. It proved unsatisfactory because it was located too far from Hillsborough and right next to a busy roundabout. That certainly had an adverse influence on our preparations.

There's no doubt that we had a good team. We also had a good strategy, which was something of a contrast to our approach in Sweden. Things didn't go as we had planned, and we were accused of playing too defensively. But that way of looking at it is rubbish in my opinion. The squad gave everything they had – all the players who were available were there and worked hard – it's just that we lacked a consistent goalscorer. A lot of forwards have been in and out of the national team in recent years; we just have to admit that Denmark is a small country which cannot always produce the really dangerous man up front, the kind of striker who can reliably capitalise on the chances we are always able to create. It's not every day that a player like Preben Elkjaer is born. Brian Laudrup was developing into a reasonably consistent goalscorer, but he is now out of the equation. The accusations about defensive play directed towards 'Ricardo' were just way off the mark.

Every year, around 26 June, the European Championship team of 1992 gets together at Ricardo's home on his native island of Funen. This has become a regular tradition. We enjoy each other's company, and bask in the glow of our conviction that our team was able to put Denmark on the international football map. We are no longer a 'nearly' nation which year after year stumbles at the finishing line. We made it to the top, and gave football-loving Danes everywhere a new and welcome identity. No one can take that away from us, and for me the roar of the jubilant crowd at the Nya Ullevi Stadium in Gothenburg on 26 June 1992 is one of the greatest experiences of my footballing career.

8 United – Life as a Professional

'Once you have a place in the Manchester United squad, you are in some way receiving a calling. You are under a lot of pressure, not just in terms of delivering on the pitch, but as a representative of some of the proudest traditions in English football. You are a part of the history, you help to carry the torch forward for a while, and you feel obliged to play your part in maintaining the spirit that pervades the club.'

'ONLY TWO BEERS EACH TONIGHT, lads!' Alex Ferguson shouted, and he wagged his finger as a warning.

We had just finished playing one of my first practice matches with Manchester United. I was slightly surprised by my new boss' words. We had just lost the game 1–5, so as far as I was concerned there was nothing to celebrate. On the other hand I could sense that there was some cultural point here that I had to grasp, something about the difference between the Danish and the English temperament. Fundamental differences in lifestyle which go to the very heart of my livelihood: professional football. It didn't take me long to get used to the fact that the number of beers allowed after a match is a central part of a footballer's life here in England. And you can hardly expect it to be otherwise in a country where the pub culture is such a deep-rooted part of everyday life.

A high proportion of English players have working-class roots, and they carry traditions with them into their footballing lives which are widely accepted. This makes life as a professional in English football a relatively relaxed affair compared with what it's like in so many other places. There is discipline, of course, just as there is at any other club around the world, but it is primarily a form of self-discipline that stems from a philosophy of freedom with responsibility. English players, broadly speaking, are very accomplished at handling themselves according to this philosophy, but for United players it seems there's an extra dimension.

Once you have a place in the Manchester United squad, you are in some way receiving a calling. You are under a lot of pressure, not just in terms of delivering on the pitch, but as a representative of some of the proudest traditions in English football. You are a part of the history, you help to carry the torch forward for a while, and you feel obliged to play your part in maintaining the spirit that pervades the club, a club founded in 1878 by a group of railway workers from the Lancashire and Yorkshire Railway Company.

When considering the history of this great club, it's difficult to avoid mentioning the blackest chapter in Manchester United's history. Much has been written about the Munich air disaster of February 1958, and it's impossible not to be affected by that tragic event because it still casts deep emotional shadows over the life of the club. United had been in Belgrade to play in the quarter-finals of the European Cup against Red Star. The game ended in a 3–3 draw, but United won the tie 5–4 on aggregate. A stop-over landing in Munich proved to be disastrous because the pilot was unable to keep the plane in the air after take-off. It crashed to the ground in thick fog, and 23 of the 44 people on board were killed. Among those killed were eight players who will forever be remembered at Old Trafford, namely the defenders Roger Byrne, Geoff Bent and Mark Jones, midfield players Eddie Colman and Duncan Edwards, and forwards Billy Whelan, Tommy Taylor and David Pegg.

The light in this darkness was that nine players survived (John Berry and Jackie Blanchflower never played again), among them Bobby Charlton, while the club's manager, Matt Busby, endured a long and hard struggle for his life at a hospital in Munich. He won his battle and returned to become one of the greatest names in the club's history. The reward for his stubborn fighting spirit was an additional 36 years of glorious service at the club.

I will never forget that day in January 1994 when the team bade a formal farewell to that great gentleman of football. We were playing against Everton, and even the weather was on Matt Busby's side: it was, despite the time of year, a bright and sunny Saturday afternoon. Forty-four thousand fans were at the ground and had sung their way through the hours leading up to kick-off in the traditional way. Then the announcer at the ground asked for silence, and as if by magic a hush descended on Old Trafford while the players were led on to the pitch by a lone bagpiper. The entire crowd rose to its feet without a sound. We all bowed our heads as a final sign of respect for one of the club's greatest men. It was a soul-stirring moment which truly embodied the essence of Manchester United, and the roar which followed the silence seemed to me to be almost supernatural in its strength.

Those were moving days at the club. Four days later we all attended the funeral at the Roman Catholic church of St John's in Chorlton, where the Bishop of Salford sent Matt Busby on his final journey with the following description: 'A humble man, whose life and death have touched the lives of thousands of people.' That was neither an understatement nor an exaggeration, because the whole basis for the life of any club is the supporters. They are the foundations of the club. The United fans create the wonderful atmosphere at Old Trafford, and they pay our wages. Sir Matt Busby understood this.

Manchester United is by no means an ordinary club. It is a giant institution, a money machine of enormous proportions at the base of which are the 100,000 official members and thousands of others who belong to United's supporters' clubs all over the world. It is a huge organisation that thrives on enthusiasm and devotion, and the players are the humble servants of this culture. It may seem slightly weird to associate the word 'humble' with the lives of highly paid professional footballers, but it's nevertheless a reality that pervades our lives, and I have never encountered it anywhere else to such an extent as at Manchester United.

It's true that we arrive in our big cars; it's true that our bank accounts are fed with considerable sums of money; and it's a fact that in the eyes of the public we are stars, to a greater or lesser degree. But those aspects of our lives occupy only a tiny part of our consciousness when we put on our boots and tie up our laces at The Cliff, ready for work, regardless of rain or snow. Hard daily training is the foundation of our success, and it's done with respect for the club and the supporters. It requires enormous self-discipline; if you don't have it, you simply cannot be a member of the team. And I mean self-discipline right down to the smallest detail. You are punctual regarding all schedules. You show the greatest consideration at all times. You work hard physically and mentally to maintain the incredibly high standards which exist at the club. And there are also obligations which apply outside normal working hours. There is no one at the club who does not live a sober and healthy life – it is very rare that Manchester United players are involved in so-called 'scandals'.

It is deeply ingrained in every player that he is the representative of a unique system that demands a very high level of effort in all respects. Routine is a necessity in order to get through a season in the toughest league in the world.

My preparations always start the day before a game. I take my afternoon nap after training, and then I conjure up something tasty in the kitchen. To Bente's great satisfaction, I love to cook. I always prepare a pasta dish the day before a game, either ordinary pasta with a meat sauce, or a lasagne.

I don't watch an awful lot of television, but there are some series I just have to see. It could hardly be otherwise when you live in a country that produces the best TV series in the world. I thoroughly enjoy *Prime Suspect, Cracker, The Bill* and *Harry Enfield and Chums.* My favourite is *Coronation Street* and the day after we won the 1998/99 Premiership I even took my family to visit the set. I also watch the news – that is a must – but often the evening ends with me stretched out on the sofa reading. I read a lot of books, not necessarily the kind of literature that stretches me intellectually, but I'm very keen on good-quality mainstream fiction. I find it deeply relaxing to read. It enriches you; sometimes you even gain a little wisdom; and if nothing else it entertains, and keeps you from thinking too much about the coming confrontation. After that I usually go to bed early. Probably earlier than most, because I have to get a good night's sleep before a game. My system demands it.

On match days, if we're playing at home, we meet at Old Trafford at midday – no earlier, no later. We eat a light lunch, fool around a lot, tease each other, watch a bit of TV and attempt to make the waiting as relaxing as possible. That is essential during weeks when we play two or three games in the space of seven days. If your adrenalin is pumping all the time, it just gets too much.

The gaffer announces the line-up and holds a tactics meeting an hour and a half before the game. This meeting can take anything from five minutes to half an hour.

About an hour before kick-off, the adrenalin starts to flow for real. You start to make your mental preparations for the task ahead, and the warm-up begins. I always get my first big kick when I run out to warm up. You taste the atmosphere. Is anything special going on? As time goes by, you develop a highly sensitive radar which gives you a very precise reading of what is going on in the ground. You can almost feel how the match is going to go. But then, of course, you can't possibly know, which is one of the charms of football. It is entirely unpredictable.

Then everything starts to tighten up when we make our way out into the players' tunnel. At that point we have reached a high level of tension. I love the feeling of deep concentration, of unity and the absolute will to win. From the moment we run out on to the pitch, everything else is shut out. People can shout, scream, sing or cheer. It means nothing. I have a thickly layered circle of concentration around me. There is just one thing left to do: I have to give both goalposts a kick. Bente says that it's a symbolic ritual which signals to my opponents that the goal is closed. I never forget to do it.

And then the game begins.

The 'third half' is always held in the players' lounge, where both teams meet after the game. This is where the real wind-down after games takes place. Football matches, especially in England, entail enormous physical exertion, after which you need to unwind in order to become more or less normal again. Almost irrespective of the result, it's always a pleasant experience. It's essential too. Players have to be 'debriefed', and sometimes defused. Football is a hard game and lots of things can happen in the course of a match that can really irritate players. An elbow in the face. A kick on the ankle. Tackles from behind which can pose a serious threat to the most precious possessions any footballer has: his legs. Not to mention all the petty quarrels that continually go on between players throughout a game, and which are really only an expression of the fact that each man desperately wants to win. All these episodes have to be dealt with, and the best way of doing so is over a pint. At these get-togethers after a game, players are able, if necessary, to re-establish personal relationships. They become friends and colleagues again after anger has flared up during the game. That's the way it has to be – and, thankfully, that's the way it is. After the third half you're ready for the next confrontation, because the atmosphere has been cleared.

When the third half is over, Bente and I usually go home. Life outside our home is very limited in many ways. Of course, we have a number of obligations to the club – receptions, meetings, celebrations and the like – which we fulfil, but other than that we don't tend to go out much. Even though people are generally very kind and nice to us, it is difficult for us to sit down at a restaurant in Manchester after a game, for example. I have a slight problem when it comes to blending into the background, and it's inevitable that people will want to have a little chat, ask me for my autograph or something like that. It's a situation I have to accept, but naturally it has its unwanted consequences: my food gets cold, for instance! So we usually just pop off home. And really it suits me fine. Relaxation is a very important element of life as a professional. There is always training again the next morning. Your muscles need to loosen up.

The next day at the training ground you have a massage, minor injuries are treated, and everyone starts to think about the next match. That is the never-ending treadmill of the professional game. It is always a question of the next match. And they hang like pearls on a thread, stretching out over the long, long season. That aspect of my profession certainly isn't glamorous: it's a long, hard grind, a question of continual, often exhausting work which is an absolute necessity if you want to reach, and stay at, the top.

Naturally, Manchester United players are well looked after.

That's obviously the way it has to be when expectations are so high. But our training ground, The Cliff, certainly couldn't be called luxurious in any way. It's so modest, in fact, that I couldn't really believe my eyes when I first saw it – couldn't square it with a club the size of Manchester United at all – but I have to admit that it serves its purposes. In all fairness, I should add that the club is currently putting the finishing touches to a brand new training facility at a cost of almost £11 million. It's due to open in January 2000.

The Cliff has all the facilities required for the running of a top football team. The club has its own dietician who makes sure that healthy food is provided. There are doctors and physiotherapists. There are people to look after the kit, boot polishers, and it's also possible to get your car washed while you're at training. The ground is completely sealed off to everyone apart from players and club staff. Players even have to leave any guests they might have with them in an anteroom. Guests are simply not allowed. The players must be permitted to go about their everyday job in peace and quiet, without distractions.

On the other hand, people are welcome to come and watch training, and a surprising number of people do take the opportunity. This has always astonished me, because training routines aren't always the most exciting things in the world to watch. But I must say that it was always heartening to see so many people there – a good expression of the loyal support that exists at Manchester United. We always had attention focused upon us; even when we left the training ground there were often large groups of supporters, including many young girls who just wanted to catch a glimpse of David Beckham, Ryan Giggs and the rest of them. As I said before, this attention is an unavoidable part of everyday life, and is really no strain at all. This is because the English are polite, almost shy, and treat their idols in a respectful, pleasant and non-aggressive way which makes contact with them very easy.

Football is, especially in England, a sport of the working classes. Your average English football fan almost by definition prefers the simpler things in life, more or less as a direct result of the level of his or her earnings, but they all have something which they devote themselves to heart and soul. This is part of the reason why angling is the most widely practised pastime in England, followed closely by football. And it is through our meetings with these devoted fans that we reap the rewards for our hard grind at the training ground. The wonderful atmosphere that exists at British grounds, which is built up in the hours before a game and – at Manchester United at any rate – is given extra backing by the thousands of people who didn't get a ticket but who follow the game outside the ground, is almost payment enough for me. English teams are very conscious of the debt they owe to their fans, and always try to pay some of it back on the pitch. They always make a 100 per cent effort. It is hectic, it is wild, it is wonderful! It is really magnificent football.

I cannot imagine that a more stimulating supporting culture exists anywhere else in the world, and that's certainly one of the things I shall miss. The fact that I have also come to value a number of other typically English characteristics very highly – for example, pride in being British, the subtle humour, not to mention the outstanding quality of television programmes – speaks for itself. In fact, one of the first things I will do in Lisbon is ensure that I can receive English television. That must be possible in this digital day and age.

Being a professional at the top also means that there's an almost never-ending supply of people who want to contact you. Our fax machine is kept busy at all hours of the day, and Bente and I often wonder how people have got hold of our number. They all manage to get through: companies, the press and ordinary people with all manner of requests, suggestions, invitations, etc. It can be difficult to keep track of it all. I have to admit that the great majority of enquiries receive a negative reply. There's a limit to how many balls you can juggle with at one time, and I'm very careful not to overload myself at the expense of my primary objectives: playing football and spending time with my family.

But from time to time I do take part in certain projects that interest me, and I have also co-operated with a number of different companies in their advertising campaigns. But money's not something I discuss. It's a private affair, and isn't all that interesting anyway. Money has never been a motivating force in my career. And, of course, there are people you must surround yourself with as a professional footballer. In chapter 16 I describe how I worked with a British management firm. In Denmark my interests are well looked after by my good friend Ole Frederiksen, and apart from that I work together with various solicitors and financial advisers – and my agent. It's an indispensable part of modern professional life.

I'm a footballer. But I'm also a company.

9 Sir Alex Ferguson

'It turned into a fight between two will-powers, neither of which was interested in or capable of backing down. I said the most awful things. I questioned his abilities as a manager. I aired doubts about his personal qualities. Ferguson didn't keep anything back either, and at one point he threatened to throw a cup of tea in my face.'

I T'S 23 APRIL 1997. In front of 53,000 spectators at Old Trafford we lose for the second time in the semi-finals of the Champions' League, at the hands of the eventual winners, Borussia Dortmund. Lars Ricken had scored as early as the eighth minute, a soft shot that took a deflection off Gary Pallister's toe, sending the ball in a curve around me and out of my reach, catching me on the wrong foot.

At half-time no comments were made about this goal in the United changing room, but after the game Alex Ferguson came up to me straight away and thundered: 'F*****g hell, Peter! F*****g easy goal to give away!' I pointed out that the ball had taken a deflection, and Pallister backed me up. Alex Ferguson accepted this immediately and later he came to me and apologised. By the time the next game arrived, Ferguson had been out and bought himself a pair of glasses. He apologised to me once again that he had been unable to see the deflection from his seat. He had subsequently checked out the incident on TV and was now convinced I was not at fault.

This episode says something fundamental about the man who is probably the best-known manager in the world at the moment: he might be a passionate and demanding man, but he is also scrupulously fair. It's fairly common knowledge that at one time – that is, before I arrived at Manchester United – he was known as 'the hair dryer' because when players didn't live up to what was expected of them at United, he would never shy away from giving them the sort of face-to-face dressing-down that would blow their hair out of place. I have experienced this myself, although on one occasion – at Anfield after a 3–3 draw with Liverpool – we were like two hair dryers that not only spoilt each other's haircuts but almost blew each other out of the changing room.

But I'll return to that episode later. Let me say at this point that my relationship with Alex Ferguson can be summed up in one word: respect. Or perhaps two words: deep respect. And I am pretty sure that he has the same attitude towards me. We have been closely tied together throughout Manchester United's heady adventures in the 1990s, ever since the day at the beginning of the decade when he paid me a visit in the Copenhagen suburb of Ishoj. It was there, at the home of Finn Villy Sorensen (my first manager), that I had my first ever conversation with the man.

When Ferguson came to Ishoj, it was already a done deal. His main reason for coming over was to meet me face-to-face and to convince me that even though we weren't able to sign on the dotted line there and then, everything was going as planned. Rune Hauge had finished the negotiations with Martin Edwards at an earlier point.

United's goalkeeping coach, Alan Hodgkinson, had been to Denmark on many occasions to check me out and had – according to Finn Villy Sorensen – returned to England after seeing me for the first time with the words: 'He's going to be a big hit in the UK.' All of Hodgkinson's visits to Denmark occurred before Ferguson came to Ishoj.

We couldn't sign a contract at that time because that very summer United were quoted on the Stock Exchange and became a plc. The club wasn't able to spend money until after 1 August 1991.

United could easily have gone back out on to the European, or English, transfer market and found a more established top-class goalkeeper, but apparently Alex Ferguson wanted me. And that was a conviction which thankfully neither of us has ever needed to regret. My eight years together with the charismatic Scot whom no one – and I mean no one – overlooks when he walks into a room, turned out to be the most successful years of my career – and so far of his, too.

The other side of this success – and I deliberately avoid calling it the reverse side – is of course the hard physical and mental strains under which both players and managers work. We live in a climate of such extreme competition that confrontations are not just unavoidable, but numerous. And they often develop as a result of the psychological ploys which Alex Ferguson is a master at initiating and manipulating.

In order to understand him, you have to know that he is an extremely proud man when it comes to his players. His faith in the team which he has built up over the last ten years or so has been enormous and unyielding. He has always been aware of what his charges are capable of and what their limitations are, and he has certainly always told them how good he thinks they all are and backed them up 100 per cent. But on the other hand he has always demanded that they give their utmost. And when, on occasion, this was not the case, he would let them know – and not always in a nice way. In fact, often in a not very nice way at all. But – and this is of fundamental importance – he never lets the sun go down on his wrath. He is not a man who bears a grudge, and for a man in his position that is a fantastic quality.

How often have you heard it said of football teams that so-and-so is on the bench for this match, or watching the game from the stands, even though everybody knows that the player in question has got what it takes to be in the team? This is almost always a question of personal friction between players and managers, where spite and grudge take over and where, in the end, the manager is forced to make clear, or even defend, his position through some demonstration of his power. This kind of thing can have a damaging effect on the player in question, and the team as a whole. I have never known Alex Ferguson to do this kind of thing. He is simply too big-hearted.

Of course, I'm not now trying to say that Alex Ferguson does not have a temper. It would be one of the great understatements of football history to claim that. Mistakes are made in every football match, and there's no avoiding them; irrespective of how well you play overall, there are always things to get excited or even downright mad about. But what is characteristic about Alex Ferguson is that he adjusts the tone and force of his complaints according to the player. He has a sophisticated and well-defined sense for who it would be appropriate to 'attack' and who he should be rather more careful with. Not everyone in the team has the same psychological strength. Ferguson knows that, and acts wisely to the benefit of the team. I have seen him storm and rage on innumerable occasions at Gary Pallister, who certainly is the kind of man on to whom he could unload things. When their quarrels were at their height in the changing room you could almost feel yourself getting concerned for their physical safety. But a few hours later the same two men would be sitting down together playing cards, joking and fooling around on the four-hour coach trip home from London. Someone who hadn't witnessed the earlier confrontation wouldn't have the slightest notion that these two guys a short while before had almost bitten each other's heads off.

After a while, as I gained more experience and played myself in at Manchester United, I, like Gary Pallister, was also given a kind of scapegoat role by Alex Ferguson. He was certain that I could take it, and even more certain that I would bite like an aggressive fish on a hook when he cast his juicy bait. It was not always pleasant, least of all at half-time when your adrenalin is on the boil, but through these arguments with me he was, for example, able to point out the things he was dissatisfied with so that everyone, without exception, understood what he meant without having to stand directly in the line of fire. I think that he deliberately tried to provoke a temper in the team that would make us naturally aggressive during games.

Back to the Anfield match I mentioned earlier, the only occasion I can remember when an argument really got out of hand – and you will perhaps not be surprised to learn that it was between Ferguson and myself. Liverpool's home ground is arguably the place where we most like to win, mainly because of all the stadiums in England it is at Anfield where Manchester United are most unpopular – not to say downright hated. After less than half an hour of the match, on 4 January 1994, we were leading 3–0 and in complete control of the game. We could have scored another five goals in the first half, but we didn't. Liverpool clawed two goals back before the break to make the score 3–2. In our swaggering self-confidence we relaxed, and from that point on we never really got into the right gear again. Liverpool dominated the rest of the game. Naturally we tried to fight our way out of the situation, but our luck had changed and we could do nothing to turn the tide. By the time the referee blew the final whistle, Liverpool had earned themselves a draw.

The game was subsequently rated as one of the best ever shown on Sky Sports, but for some reason that didn't impress Alex Ferguson. He wasn't just livid, he was absolutely hysterical, and the first thing he did when we got into the changing room was to launch a seething verbal attack on me over the quality of my goal kicks. He didn't just criticise some of my goal kicks, he more or less heaped derision on *all* the goal kicks I had taken in the entire game. I was speechless. I felt that he was blaming the result on me, and it seemed to me – although it was probably a bit of an exaggeration – that in the second half I had been forced to take a goal kick or to clear my area about once every twenty seconds. That's some indication of the amount of pressure we put ourselves under, and for me in such a situation there is only one course of action: get the ball as far up into the opposition's half as possible. Naturally, most of my kicks landed on the heads of Liverpool's central defenders – it could hardly be otherwise.

I found out that evening that Ferguson's frustration actually had nothing whatsoever to do with my goal kicks – I was just a convenient sounding-board again – but was related to something much more fundamental: the fact that we had played excellent, almost dreamlike football for 45 minutes and then allowed ourselves to fall apart. We had made fools of ourselves in the stadium of our great Merseyside rivals, and if there is one thing that can really upset Ferguson – and me, for that matter – it is slackness that leads to humiliation.

For that reason it was an unfortunate evening for him to launch an attack on me. I was angry myself! How can a good football team throw away a 3–0 lead and not be able to do a single thing about it? That was the question I was asking myself when Ferguson started to attack me.

At this point I lost control of myself, and I would imagine that in the calmer and more reasonable light of reflection he would agree with me that neither of us truly meant what followed: a gigantic argument which with the speed of lightning reached such a personal level that I don't care to mention what was said. That's how embarrassing it was. It turned into a fight between two will-powers, neither of which was interested in or capable of backing down. I said the most awful things. I questioned his capabilities as a manager. I aired doubts about his personal qualities. Ferguson didn't keep anything back either, and at one point he threatened to throw a cup of tea in my face. In the end I just turned my back on him and headed for the showers, embarrassingly aware of the fact that it had grown deadly silent in the changing room. No one felt like saying anything at all, and certainly no one wanted to risk any action that might end in his involvement in that ridiculous scene.

That row is legend today, one of the episodes the players most often recall when they have a laugh and tell old stories. But at the time there was nothing funny about it all. I was furious when I drove home, and I rang my agent, Rune Hauge, to ask him to find me a new club. And to find one straight away!

By the next day I had calmed down a bit, but on my way to training I was still thinking seriously about my future at the club. I knew that the incident was bound to have repercussions in one way or another, and I was mentally prepared for the fact that my adventures with Manchester United might be coming to an end. To be quite honest, this was not a thought that pleased me very much, but I knew I had to face up to the consequences of my behaviour like a man. In fact, the only person who was not present at training that day was Alex Ferguson, so it turned out to be a day where nothing was settled. I am quite sure that his absence that day had nothing to do with his row with me; as I have already pointed out, Alex Ferguson is not a man to avoid a confrontation.

The day after that, however, he was there. I went to see him in his office. He asked me to sit down, looked at me for a while and said: 'I suppose you realise that I have no choice but to give you the sack?'

Of course, I was prepared for this. I braced myself, and asked: 'From when?'

'I'll have to figure that out,' he replied. 'But the main thing for now is that we are professionals. We have a game coming up and you're playing on Saturday. But the fact that we are professionals also means that I can't have a player who allows himself to talk to me like that. I suppose you understand that?'

'I know that. I'm sorry about it and I'd like to give you an unconditional apology.'

'I accept it, but of course it doesn't alter the fact that you'll have to leave.'

So I was fired by the time I went down to the other players, who stood waiting, partly for me to come back from his office to read my expression, and partly for Alex Ferguson to arrive for a run-through of the Liverpool game.

The post-mortem went off quietly, although he was naturally still a bit bad-tempered about the fact that we had allowed ourselves to commit the greatest sin of all: to relax in a highly favourable situation – and against Liverpool, no less – and by doing so throw away two championship points.

After he had gone, and my team-mates were also about to leave, I asked them to stay. I gave a short improvised speech which went something like this: 'Lads, I owe you an apology for my behaviour after the game. It was childish of me; embarrassing and unforgivable. Naturally, I've given the boss an apology, but it wasn't him who asked me to do this. I just feel that I owe you all an apology.' They were all happy to accept it, but what I didn't know was that Alex Ferguson was standing just outside the door and had heard every word. I was told this by Rune Hauge later on. Ferguson had discussed the matter with him and had been really surprised that I was able to eat my words – and swallow my pride – in this way. And perhaps that was the reason why my verbal sacking never materialised as a formal notice of dismissal.

It is worth mentioning that although he is renowned for his temper, Ferguson has grown a good deal calmer over the years. Also, it was never the case that he would go berserk after every game or during every interval. Interestingly, it wasn't uncommon for him to vent his spleen after a victory during which some slack play caught his attention and the need to point it out overwhelmed him.

The gaffer and I never mentioned this matter again, and, typically for him, it has never cast any shadows on what in all other respects has been a great relationship which has helped lead Manchester United to the top and culminated in us winning the Treble in 1999. This was to a great extent Ferguson's accomplishment, and I think it fulfilled his dream of a lifetime. He has guided Manchester United through what is undoubtedly their most successful season ever. It stands as one of the greatest achievements in football history, and it will never be forgotten in a country that understands how to pay tribute to its heroes, and does so with all its heart.

Ferguson's story is a fantastic one. Born into extremely modest surroundings, he never became a really great footballer himself (he is going to love me for this!), although he did enjoy several seasons with Glasgow Rangers before being given his first job as a manager at the early age of 32. But in his chosen profession he has really understood how to make every pound count. The secret behind his success, in addition to an iron will, has very simply been work, work and more work.

At our daily training sessions at Manchester United, I was always one of the first players to arrive at the ground. As my parking place was right beside Alex Ferguson's, I was never in doubt about his working hours. I used to arrive every day around nine o'clock, and when I parked my car alongside his, I could always be sure that its bonnet was already cold. He had been there for a long time! His office, a very modest affair, contained a table, two chairs and a book case. But a TV and video recorder totally dominated the room. Video tapes were everywhere. Here he almost constantly checked recorded games featuring future opponents. And he didn't just run these tapes once; they were often played through three, four, even five times before he was satisfied he'd absorbed all the relevant information. Afterwards, he was in a position to plan our tactics and to point out with astonishing precision which 'holes' existed in the defence systems of our next opponents; their running patterns were analysed down to the slightest detail; every possible way of confusing them was pinpointed; every weak, or just uncertain, piece of marking had our attention drawn to it. After that it was up to us to utilise this knowledge bestowed upon us. Ferguson would also always have a scout at the stadiums. The next day he would receive a report about ten pages long which in tireless detail – and here we are talking about seriously minor details – described the game in question, together with an up-to-the-minute evaluation of each of the players.

As a result of Ferguson's industry there was always extensive material available to the United players. But we always had a slightly ambivalent attitude towards these 'recipes for success', because when it came down to it, we were the team who played their own game. We sought out the artistic side of the game of football, taking both necessary and often also unnecessary chances based on the belief that we could always score one more goal than our opponents. This was a blind but psychologically refined faith implanted in us by Alex Ferguson, which often – and sometimes in the final phase of a game, where our greatness really sparkled – enabled us to get the better of opponents who were mistakenly under the impression that Manchester United were beaten. Just look at the last half of the season in 1999: we didn't lose a single game. Admittedly, we drew some, but that didn't prevent us from achieving the greatest of all triumphs: Premier League champions, FA Cup winners and victors in the Champions' League in the same season.

It was an incredible feat, and yet, for many of us, an expected reward for the solid development of a team which Alex Ferguson had guided with expertise and an iron hand, not just through attention to detail and the acquisition of new players, but by means of a constant and very determined belief that it was his team, and no other, that would be able to produce dreamlike football when it was absolutely necessary. His knighthood, placing him on a par with giants like Sir Bobby Charlton, is fully deserved, and a magnificent triumph. He came from the backstreets of Glasgow. His will-power drove him on, all the way, and I know that he is tremendously proud of his title.

And I have no problem whatsoever with addressing him accordingly. Sir Alex, you have my utmost respect!

10 Eric Cantona – The King

'On one occasion he was dressed in a black dinner suit, a white open-necked shirt – and a pair of red Nike trainers. It looked a little comical, and it certainly made a bit of a stir. Actually, I thought it looked quite cool – and it took a lot of guts. Another time, he turned up in an Indian robe, which also looked good on him. His way of thinking was simply that, under the majority of circumstances, he did what he liked. He didn't worry at all about what people might think of him.'

T HERE ARE NO BAD PLAYERS at a club like Manchester United. Everyone, irrespective of his position and role in the team, maintains a fantastically high standard both physically and mentally. Otherwise there is no room for him. All the same, there are those who represent something extraordinary, something sublime. Not just as a result of individual performances on the pitch, but because they are blessed with the talent to inspire and pull everyone else together.

Eric Cantona belonged in this category. To use a slightly worn-out cliché, he made all the difference. By means of his own mental energy – and his ingenious footballing skills – he gave Manchester United an extra five per cent. The club's domestic record clearly shows that from the moment he pulled on the famous red shirt in December 1992, we won the championship four out of five times (this should really have been five out of five) as well as winning the FA Cup twice, beating Chelsea 4–0 in 1994 and Liverpool 1–0 in 1996.

Ironically, the mercurial Frenchman came to the club more or less by accident, although Alex Ferguson had undoubtedly kept an eye on him while he was at Leeds – a club he had also enriched and helped to become champions the season before he joined United. The version of the story I heard was that the Leeds manager, Howard Wilkinson, rang Alex Ferguson and asked him if he could buy Denis Irwin. Ferguson told him that it was out of the question, but while he had Wilkinson on the line he thought he might as well take the opportunity to enquire after the availability of Eric Cantona. To Ferguson's great surprise, Wilkinson agreed on the spot to let the player go. The price was just £1 million, and more or less the following day Eric Cantona arrived at Manchester United. There he stood, broad-shouldered, with his chest stuck out in that characteristic posture that reflected not only his strong build, but that enormous reserve of mental and physical strength with the help of which he was destined to sweep all opposition aside in the seasons to come.

From that day, Manchester United's style of play changed. Our leader had arrived, the uncrowned king of the team was in our midst, and he carried himself accordingly. Not because he was in any way stuck-up, snobbish or aloof; in fact, quite the opposite was the case: he was a highly intelligent man, both on and off the field, and in addition to that an immensely nice bloke. Nonetheless, from the very start he was conscious of the fact that it was not his job to dash half the length of the pitch to fetch the ball. That was up to others.

In his assumed role, acting as a link between the midfield and the front runners, he was unfailingly competent and often brilliant, constantly feeding his team-mates with inventive ideas and moves which were executed with technical skill and delicate style. Cantona was a two-footed player. Strong as an ox, he could leap prodigiously with two defenders on his back, bring the ball under control with his chest and slip it on through openings that no one else on the pitch had realised were there. With Cantona as our ingenious kingpin – and we certainly mustn't forget his formidable ability as a goalscorer who on innumerable occasions secured for us a one-nil victory, which is just as valuable as any other win (Cantona and I had a standing agreement which went more or less as follows: 'Peter, I score one and you keep a clean sheet, OK?') – United quickly made the transition from a strong, promising team into a distinctly great one.

If the arrival of Cantona suddenly made it clear to the coaching staff exactly how the team should play to be successful, that is not to say that everything sailed along smoothly. It actually doesn't take much psychological discord to begin to make a good team less effective, and to prevent this from happening to United Paul Ince just had to be weeded out. There is no doubt at all that Ince was, and is, a good player. But at the same time I felt he was, to put it mildly, self-centred and arrogant, and his potentially adverse influence on young players in particular was something that I know worried Alex Ferguson. Ince always referred to himself as the 'Guv'nor' – in other words, the boss – and he played up to this self-assertion to an almost absurd degree: he had GUV written on his boots, and had a number plate made with L8 GUV on it. In the end Alex Ferguson became so fed up with it that he was prompted to utter the words: 'I'll show him who the f*****g Guv is!' And he sold him to Inter Milan. From then on the atmosphere within the club simply changed, and the team improved considerably as a result.

There are perhaps many people who rate Cantona as a natural talent, which of course he was, but the secret behind his ability was an enormous amount of dedication to hard work at training, where he incessantly and patiently practised his game's little details and tricks, often after the rest of us had finished for the day. But he was never entirely alone. The young players who were at that time on their way up – Paul Scholes, Nicky Butt, Gary Neville – used to stand there and watch the big Frenchman's ball juggling – out of admiration, naturally, but also as a means of enhancing their own footballing development. They checked him out, then tried to reproduce the wide variety of specialities he was capable of serving up. In my opinion, Eric Cantona's importance to Manchester United should not be measured solely by his exploits on the Old Trafford pitch, but also on the basis of his innate ability to inspire and the desire for experimentation he instilled on the training ground.

He did possess an overwhelming arrogance – and here I use the word in a positive, not a negative, way – together with a kind of self-confidence which meant that even if his elevated style did not immediately click, he would try again, completely unruffled, until suddenly things fell into place. And when they did, his play became fluent, magical and surprising, filled with elegance; at such times I used to stand there in my goal and delight in the way in which the thrill of a successfully executed move would simply transfuse itself into the whole team and strengthen us – and, we often felt, make us almost invincible.

In fact, in terms of shortcomings, there are really only two things which spring to my mind. I would never claim that Eric was slow, but he was certainly no Michael Owen, something of which he himself was quite aware. He compensated for this lack of speed with incredible physical strength, but there was nothing to redress the balance when it came to his formidable temper, which undoubtedly gave him serious problems all through his career and which, unfortunately, reached its destructive peak while he was at Manchester United.

I will certainly never forget that Wednesday evening in January 1995 at Selhurst Park when we met Crystal Palace.

It started out as a completely ordinary football match, and stayed that way until early in the second half the ball was played back to me on the left-hand side of the goal area. I kicked the ball upfield on the left, a clearance which was aimed at Eric. He couldn't quite reach it, and I think he was so frustrated by this that he kicked out at Palace defender Richard Shaw. But he didn't touch him – at least as far as I could see! Referee Alan Wilkie reacted to Cantona's rash behaviour by sending him off, and that should have been the end of the matter. But the incident escalated dramatically as Cantona was leaving the pitch. A Crystal Palace fan by the name of Matthew Simmons came rushing down from the twentieth row and, standing at the advertising hoardings, taunted the already irritated Frenchman with the words: 'Go back to France, you f*****g French b*****d!'

On hearing this, Eric Cantona simply exploded. From my goal I saw the fiery Frenchman immediately turn around and, almost in the same second as he caught sight of the man who was shouting the abuse, launch himself into a run-up which ended with a fully-fledged karate kick to the man's chest. I think that in the ensuing fracas he also managed to slap Simmons in the face.

I was immediately aware of the fact that in the space of

these few seconds Cantona had not just managed to get himself into trouble up to his neck, but that he was over his head in the mire. I rushed up the pitch to get hold of my team-mate, who had already been almost overpowered by attendants and other players. We got him out of the mêlée and he was escorted to the changing room by Norman Davies, our kit assistant. Cantona then fully realised the gravity of the situation. He just sat there on the bench with his face buried in his hands, shaking his head, slightly amazed at the violence of his reaction.

Later on, when the incident was well behind us and Eric had served out his punishment, we sometimes teased Norman Davies, who is one of the nicest blokes on earth, with the fact that it was really his fault that Cantona had landed among the spectators. We used to tell him that if he had only held on to Eric properly to start off with when they were on their way to the changing room, none of this would have happened!

Almost instantly this incident became world-famous as TV pictures of the episode were naturally beamed all over the globe and run in slow motion again and again. It certainly wasn't a pretty sight. Of course it's totally unacceptable that spectators who have paid to see a football match should be attacked in this way, but still I couldn't help both feeling sorry for Eric and empathising to a certain extent with his fit of anger. It is a highly ignorant and provocative thing to do to mock a player with racist remarks in a situation where his temper is already extremely fragile and vulnerable, and it should be remembered that footballers are also emotional human beings and that they too deserve a reasonable amount of respect from those in the stands.

The episode created an intense furore, not just at United, but also at the Football Association, in the press and, not least, at a later date, within the English legal system. The club almost immediately realised that a disciplinary measure – preferably severe – was the best way to attempt to pacify outraged public opinion. In this way United could demonstrate that they took the matter very seriously, and at the same time it was naturally hoped that a severe punishment would let some of the hot air out of the enormous balloon of indignation which had very quickly been inflated by the FA. And the sentence was pronounced quickly: Eric Cantona was suspended for four months, in effect for the remainder of the season, which meant that he would miss sixteen League matches. He was left, however, with the possibility of training with the first-team squad and playing in the reserves, if he wished to do so. In addition United forced him to pay a fine of £20,000.

The FA were a little more strict. They suspended Cantona until 1 October – nearly two months into the new season – and also fined him £8,000. FIFA also took action in the matter by giving the Frenchman an international suspension to prevent him from avoiding the ban by changing club. At the same time Eric lost his place in the French national side – he had been captain. In other words, a number of severe sanctions were enforced by the game's authorities. His punishment was given a new dimension when the judge at East Croydon magistrates court sentenced Eric to fourteen days in jail for assault. This was a shocking scenario for the Frenchman, who off the pitch had always been a well-balanced character. He literally turned quite pale when he was faced with the prospect of being put behind bars, but the club's lawyers successfully appealed and the sentence was commuted to 120 days' community service, which he served by coaching young boys and girls at the United training ground.

I felt very badly about the whole thing. First of all, it was a clear handicap for us to have to do without our general for so long. Furthermore, in my opinion Eric was unfairly subjected to a negative form of special treatment – simply because he was a high-profile footballer. If this incident had taken place in a pub, the people involved would have got away with a warning or a fine at the most. Naturally an episode like this generates a great deal of debate, and I admit that on that January evening Cantona brought the game of football into disrepute with his uncontrolled and ill-judged behaviour, but it seems to me that no attention whatsoever was paid to obviously mitigating circumstances. The repercussions of this incident were out of proportion to the crime, and Eric Cantona can only thank his own strength of mind for the fact that he was capable of returning to football at the highest level after serving his ban.

In actual fact, he was a better player on his return to the top flight. When he finally began to play again, he quickly demonstrated that he had learned how to control his temper, and I think he only had his name taken three times in the rest of his career. This must be considered something of an achievement compared with the number of yellow cards he had been awarded prior to that night at Selhurst Park.

Of course, it wasn't the first time that this controversial Frenchman had plunged himself headlong into a conflict. You could say that he had a list of sins that would have put a hardened criminal in the shade. I don't intend to go into them here because this isn't the right place, but I've always wondered what kind of forces he has inside him that occasionally set off these wild outbursts. When you're together with him in the normal course of events, he is a well-informed, quiet man who is particularly interested in art and literature. He is level-headed and witty, easy-going to the extreme, and his behaviour towards other people is immaculate. I know this perfectly well, because I have shared hotel rooms with him on several trips, and the times we had together were most enjoyable.

When he arrived from Leeds he spoke very little English. Of course, he had a basic knowledge, but it wasn't possible to get into a real conversation with him. He craved solitude, really enjoying his own company without at the same time being unpleasantly stand-offish. It was just an accepted fact among the players and staff that he more or less went his own way. The fact that he had a very acute ear for language was something I didn't find out until later. He actually learned to speak very good English in the end, but he kept this ability to himself for a long time. I think perhaps he did that in order to protect himself and to make sure that he didn't get involved in too much. It wasn't really his style – he was a loner.

When it came down to it, in fact, from what I saw he was

completely uninterested in football – apart from when he was playing himself. Of course, he could take part in an intellectual discussion about tactics and strategy, but you never saw him hanging around in front of a TV to watch a game. He was an individualist, which he often demonstrated in his own quiet but unmistakable way. He never, for instance, attempted to adjust to English customs – with regard to dressing habits and his behaviour in general.

Every time Manchester United win something, there is usually a reception to attend – as a rule deadly boring, but it is all part of the set-up. In England, you wear a shirt and tie on such occasions. Anything else is unthinkable. But not for Eric Cantona, who arrived at several of these gatherings in clothing which, to put it mildly, caused quite a sensation. On one occasion he was dressed in a black dinner suit, a white open-necked shirt – and a pair of red Nike trainers. It looked a little comical, and it certainly made a bit of a stir. Actually, I thought it looked quite cool – and it took a lot of guts. Another time, he turned up in an Indian robe, which also looked good on him. His way of thinking was simply that he, under the majority of circumstances, did what he liked. He didn't worry at all about what people might think of him.

This idea of freedom of expression was something he exploited to the full, both on and off the pitch. But by 1997 it was all over. As befitted the man, the ending of his footballing career smacked of his individualism: he simply decided that he would prefer a life outside the world of football. He got himself involved in film and theatre production in France, and as far as I know he very rarely visits England these days.

He is still missed at United. He is missed by the crowd, who loved him; by the players, who learned so much from him; and by the directors, who seem to have acknowledged that they will never again be able to acquire such an influential player at such a low price.

It would simply be impossible.

11 The Ian Wright Episode

'I had just saved a shot, and was lying on the ground holding the ball when I saw Ian Wright come flying madly towards me feet-first, with his studs showing. I sensed what was going to happen next and was concerned that the resulting collision was likely to end up breaking my leg, or at least give me a serious injury. Luckily, his first foot struck the ball initially and this took some of the power out of the contact with my shin, but had the ball and shinpad not been there, my leg would most certainly have been broken. While I buckled up with the pain, Ian Wright left the scene of the crime without so much as a word.'

'HOW DARE YOU CALL ME a black b*****d, you racist pig!' The words struck me like the crack of a whip, and they were repeated over and over again.

Ian Wright, who was at that time an Arsenal forward, was screaming at me in the players' tunnel as we left the pitch at Highbury after having beaten the London club 2–1 on 19 February 1997. I was both livid and quite cold with shock at the same time, and as the Arsenal striker hurled unwarranted accusations at me – a continuation of the contretemps between us at Old Trafford three months earlier when the two teams had last met in the League – I was being escorted by a policeman, just like Wright was, because we had had a confrontation directly after the final whistle.

I proceeded quietly towards the dressing room. Once inside the atmosphere was one of heated outrage at Ian Wright's behaviour towards me, both on the field and in the players' tunnel. We discussed whether we should launch an attack on him and his antics to the members of the press who were waiting outside. Several of us really felt like doing so, so it was probably a good thing that the journalists had left the stadium by the time we finally got out of the changing room. At that moment I didn't realise that I was about to experience one of the most difficult and ugly periods in the whole of my footballing career.

In the months that followed I felt I was led a merry dance not just by Ian Wright and the British tabloid press, but also by the General Secretary of the Football Association at that time, Graham Kelly, and – even more absurdly, given the outcome of this episode – by the chairman of the PFA, Gordon Taylor. The fact that the police also carried out a lengthy investigation concerning the racist remarks I was alleged to have made at the expense of Ian Wright – for which, I'd like to make clear from the outset, the Crown Prosecution Service never found any reason to take me to court – gives some indication of the magnitude of the issue and the pressure I was under. I was literally on the brink of being the first player in the history of the Premier League to be charged with racist behaviour. Luckily, it didn't go that far. But if it had, it would have been the most grievous injustice I have ever experienced.

As we had an away game three days after the Highbury encounter, against Chelsea, the whole squad stayed on in London, and when I got back to my hotel room I had a strange feeling, stirrings prompted by some kind of sixth sense. I decided to write down what I had experienced at the game. I didn't really know why I was doing it, but I had a feeling that it might help me later on, and this turned out to be correct. This is exactly what I wrote on my computer:

The game itself was reasonably quiet, until we got into the last thirty minutes. However, there had been a couple of episodes in the first half. The first shot at my goal was deflected, and the ball ran towards the corner flag on the right, but in order to be certain I dived to cover it on its way out. Ian Wright also followed the ball up, and it seemed to me he purposely ran into me while I was lying on the ground. I ignored this. I didn't want to give him any satisfaction on that account. The second episode was more spectacular, and, I thought, quite amusing. The ball was played up on Arsenal's right wing, and I ran out to clear it. Ian Wright also went for the ball, and it ended in a tackle that was so powerful that the ball was literally punctured! I had a bit of a laugh, but Ian Wright was completely stony-faced.

But the first half had been a disappointing affair both for Arsenal and for Ian Wright. They were losing 2–0, and Wright had wasted two good chances. From the bench Alex Ferguson had sensed that Wright's famous inner volcano was about to erupt, and before we went out for the second half he warned us: 'Don't get involved with Wright, he's about to crack.'

This analysis proved to be quite correct. First he hacked down Denis Irwin, and was correctly awarded a yellow card. Then followed what I consider to be the most serious and most brutal attack perpetrated on an English football pitch this season. I had just saved a shot, and was lying on the ground holding the ball when I saw Ian Wright come flying madly towards me feet-first, with his studs showing. I sensed what was going to happen next and was concerned that the resulting collision was likely to end up breaking my leg, or at least give me a serious injury. Luckily, his first foot struck the ball initially and this took some of the power out of the contact with my shin, but had the ball and my shinpad not been there, my leg would most certainly have been broken. While I buckled up in pain, Ian Wright left the scene of the crime without so much as a word, and quite frankly I was amazed at and disgusted by his conduct.

That's not the kind of incident you just forget about. When the game was over I ran up to him and said, 'You tried to get me!'

He just glowered at me, and replied, 'F**k off, you Danish w****r!'

'But that's what you were trying to do!'

'F**k off!' he shouted, getting increasingly worked up.

This little exchange resulted in the two policemen pulling us apart and escorting us individually down the players' tunnel, but their presence didn't prevent Ian Wright from continuing to shout at me. To start off with he used ordinary, everyday insults, but then came the words which shocked me to the core: 'How dare you call me a black b*****d, you racist pig!' He went on and on, and I was shaking with fury. First of all, I had never shouted racist remarks at him, and secondly, I understood intuitively that he was simply trying to draw attention away from his attack on me in the most cynical and irresponsible way. I immediately sensed that this might develop into a major issue.

And that was the account I wrote down that night.

I didn't have to wait long for the sparks of controversy to fly. The very next morning I found out that the Football Association, completely on its own initiative, had issued a press statement which was broadcast on London radio news. It read: 'Manchester United's goalkeeper, Peter Schmeichel, runs the risk of being charged as a result of the allegations that Ian Wright has made against him concerning racist comments in connection with the games between Manchester United and Arsenal on 16 November 1996 [at Old Trafford] and 19 February 1997 [Highbury].'

When I heard that I realised that a football-politics carousel had spun into motion. I had two options: I could jump on to the merry-go-round and take an active part in the furious debate that would surely follow, defending my corner against all-comers; or I could simply keep out of it and put the matter entirely in the hands of Manchester United's director and legal adviser, Maurice Watkins. I decided upon the latter, wiser course. And after I had made up my mind I made a very deliberate effort to keep out of the debate which came barrelling along with all the unpredictable force of a tornado. I knew that I was innocent of the charges, and I was more or less certain that my honour and my good reputation would not be spoilt by a violent campaign against me. So I chose to keep quiet, but always knowing in my heart of hearts that I would tell my side of the story at a later date. And that is what I am doing now.

But before I go back to Old Trafford in November 1996, where my alleged racist behaviour was first supposed to have taken place, I would like to give a brief description of my attitude and feelings towards Ian Wright.

There can be no doubt about the fact that he was a great striker. He was as quick as lightning, dangerous in front of goal and always aggressive, and for these reasons he was highly rated in the Arsenal team at that time. There was always something happening when he was on the pitch, but to be quite honest I have always considered him to be a bit of an idiot. There have been several disciplinary actions against him for bringing the game into disrepute, but for some reason or another he has always managed to wriggle his way out of anything resembling punishment, and I have never been able to understand why. In my opinion his vulgar behaviour should have been stamped out a long time ago.

What gives him the right to call referees 'little Hitlers'? If that isn't as tasteless as a racist remark, how else do you classify it? From my point of view he is a national bigot who thinks he can do whatever he likes. In my mind, he's an often insolent man who seems to take pleasure from sailing close to the wind, but – and this cannot be ignored – he also possesses a kind of strategic intelligence which he knows how to use to his own advantage.

The result of this is that, even before he has finished his football career, he has his own prime-time TV show, *Friday Night's All Wright*, during which he surrounds himself with famous people. While this furore raged, many people suggested that Ian Wright and I should appear in public and more or less slap each other on the back and apologise for our childish behaviour. I pointed out that he could simply invite me to appear on his TV show, but, for a number of good reasons, nothing ever came of that. But when it really comes down to the nub of the matter, I have to emphasise that I have fewer scores to settle with Ian Wright than I have with the bureaucratic leaders of the Football Association and the PFA, who were the ones I felt really let me down when it mattered.

But back to football, and Old Trafford on 16 November 1996 when we met Arsenal in front of a full house – and where the whole unfortunate affair started. In all honesty we were lucky to win 1–0 through an own goal by Nigel Winterburn, but at the end of the first half Ian Wright and I had a clash which proved to be a major catalyst in what happened later. The ball was played deep into our half to Wright, and I went out, dived and gained possession of the ball in a situation which was perhaps 70–30 in my favour. Ian Wright didn't see it that way and his studs ended up in my hand. This was very painful, and I rose to my feet straight away and gave him a real mouthful. The referee intervened immediately and pushed Ian Wright away, moments later giving him a well-deserved warning.

While the referee was talking to Wright, I stood patiently about ten yards away waiting to take the free kick. Wright was complaining vociferously about being spoken to about the foul, which in my view was gratuitous and dangerous. What I was not aware of was the fact that a TV camera was focused on me while I was standing there muttering to myself, as you do in the aftermath of a shocking experience in which you feel yourself to be the victim. I didn't address myself in any way to Ian Wright, but one TV viewer was so convinced of his own abilities as a lip-reader that he reported me to the police and the Football Association, absolutely certain that I had uttered the words 'f*****g black b*****d'.

After being reported to the police and the Football Association, the matter largely took its own course. And Ian Wright did not waste any time in scoring a bit of extra publicity. At the end of November he gave the *News of the World* an 'exclusive' interview in which I believe he abandoned all reason in a hypocritical attack on me. After having explained, first of all, how hurt and upset he was after my so-called outburst at Old Trafford, he was quoted as follows: 'What can you say about a person who apparently has such great problems about something as trivial as the colour of another person's skin?' In addition to this he also said something very interesting which we at Manchester United immediately latched on to: 'I have seen a video of the incident, and, to put it mildly, it was not very pleasant.'

That last sentence, in particular, was central to the whole case, because it implied that Ian Wright had not in fact heard what I had said on the pitch, and that he was basing his recollection of events on a combination of video evidence and an anonymous viewer's self-proclaimed talent for lip-reading. This argument – together with other aspects of the matter which were open to interpretation – was presented by our legal adviser, Maurice Watkins, to the Football Association, who had asked for our comments concerning Ian Wright's accusation. After this things went quiet – very quiet – and I thought, quite honestly, that the whole thing had met a natural and fitting end.

How naive I was. It returned with full force after the subsequent meeting between Ian Wright and myself, and our respective teams, at Highbury. On hearing the Football

Association's public announcement of the statement, which revealed that police enquiries were being carried out concerning my alleged racist outburst, I was fully aware that the matter had now become irrevocably tied up in the politics of football, and that a scapegoat would be sought. For the bureaucrats there was a straightforward solution to the problem: it was simply a question of persuading me to join the Football Association's 'Let's Kick Racism out of Football' campaign.

There were a good number of reasons why I didn't have the slightest intention of getting involved in this. It was not because I had any problem at all with supporting the main aim of this campaign – which is undoubtedly worthwhile – rather that I had no wish whatsoever to be made the focal point for a campaign of any kind. At one point, the Football Association wanted Ian Wright and I to appear together in a picture shaking hands, and all the rest of that public-relations malarkey, but again I simply refused to be a part of it. My cooperation in these schemes would have been tantamount to admitting that I really had behaved in a racist way and was now repentant. This would have given a completely false picture to the general public of the encounters I had had with Ian Wright and the fundamental view which I possess regarding other human beings.

As the case developed, it was a great help that a number of my team-mates spoke out to the press in support of me. For example, Andy Cole, who is always aware of racist tendencies of any kind on the field of play and in the stands, stated firmly that he had never experienced the slightest hint of racism from me. My former team-mate Paul Parker, with whom I had always shared rooms on our away trips, did the same, and these interventions on my behalf certainly warmed my heart.

But naturally this could not undo the feeling of injustice at the hands of the FA and the PFA that Manchester United and I laboured under. As the correspondence regarding the case grew, it became clear to both Watkins and myself, as we were forced to discuss the matter several times a day, that the FA was working according to a different agenda. The FA mandarins appeared to have decided to use me as a sacrificial offering in their anti-racism campaign. As time went by and we rejected their compromises, I felt their approaches to us were becoming increasingly rude.

Without any thought as to the consequences, I believe, they released internal and private correspondence about the matter to the press and attempted to force me to participate in joint statements, in which I was to express sincere regret about my own behaviour – and thus, again, admit that I had been lying all along and that I had hurled racist abuse at a fellow player. But on this point I remained completely firm. I would not be a pawn in a political game, and, irrespective of how much pressure was put on us, I stood my ground. I had not made racist remarks, and I am not, by any stretch of the imagination, a racist. I believe that it is important in this life that you are true to yourself and maintain a happy balance; if you are a racist, you have hate inside yourself.

Fortunately, I received 100 per cent support from the club throughout this torrid time, and Maurice Watkins knew how to keep ice-cool, which was a huge boon. With his sharp legal brain, he was able continually to undermine the arguments put forward in the FA's letters, to the point that eventually they began to run out of real evidence. When we finally agreed on a compromise, a statement that everyone could accept, it was in fact a piece of paper almost completely lacking in content, the main outcome of which was that it allowed Graham Kelly an opportunity to wag his finger at me and walk away.

This mild reprimand didn't affect me, but nevertheless Watkins and I felt that we might as well play our final trump. In a concluding letter, Watkins pulled the FA's statement apart, and we thought it necessary to emphasise the following point: 'Peter Schmeichel intends to continue to behave as he has always done, as a responsible professional footballer. As far as he is concerned, he has not received any "bad marks" for his conduct, and he intends, should it be necessary, to produce strong arguments against any allegations to the contrary.' That was our final say in the matter. The FA never replied to our comments, and I was therefore cleared of the serious accusations which had turned my life into a nightmare for a couple of months. I am pleased that the matter ended at that point, in spite of the opposition we encountered from a number of those involved.

In my opinion, Graham Kelly handled the issue in a manner ill-befitting a man in his position. I never found him particularly competent and I welcomed the news later that year that he had been replaced as General Secretary.

I haven't met Ian Wright since the storm blew itself out, which doesn't really bother me too much. I was certainly not unhappy about being absent (with leave) from Old Trafford in January 1999, when we played against West Ham, Ian Wright's new club. I was on holiday in Barbados, and was therefore spared the play-to-the-gallery speech which Ian Wright gave to the assembled media: 'This was the last time that Peter Schmeichel and I were to play against each other, and I had looked forward to shaking his hand. It would have meant a lot to me to be able say goodbye to such a great man as him on the pitch in the right way, now that he is leaving English football.' That was not a quote I particularly enjoyed reading. On the other hand, I am satisfied with the fact that the Arsenal goal-poacher never succeeded in scoring against me in a League match. I would not claim here that that was the only reason for what, over the years, amounted to a number of clashes between us, but all the same it is a statistic I am proud of, and one that can only be a source of frustration to Ian Wright.

I was more satisfied with a quote from the *Mirror*'s football expert, Mike Walters, who at the right time and in the right place wrote the following: 'If Peter Schmeichel happens to sneeze on the pitch tomorrow, I suppose he will be accused of spreading the plague.' I think that sums up my feelings pretty succinctly. The entire affair in a nutshell.

12 Red Devils

'In my opinion, Keane is British football's greatest midfield player. He's incredibly vociferous and aggressive; his almost superhuman willpower makes him enormously valuable to the team. Earlier on in his career he sustained a really serious knee injury, an injury that only allows many players to get back perhaps 80 per cent joint mobility. Not Roy Keane. He changed as a player after the injury. He began to direct and distribute brilliantly, and was invariably in the right place at the right time.'

F RIENDSHIPS DON'T EXACTLY FLOURISH in top-class football. This may well come as a surprise to people outside the game, who are used to seeing players joyfully embracing one another when a goal is scored or an important match won, but this is just an expression of the euphoria of the moment. When the gates close after a big match and the stadium lights are switched off, or training is over for the day, then the day's work is done, and most professional footballers (there are exceptions, of course) go home to their wives and kids and a life with friends who frequently have nothing to do with football at all. That's the way it is for me, and I know the same applies to many of my colleagues. A football club is a normal workplace in that sense, and life goes on there just as it does anywhere else.

Having said that, players in an elite team do become incredibly close. Mutual respect is required in order to be able to play in a way that's beneficial to the team and the club. There's nothing more poisonous for a team than irreversible or unresolved conflict between players, and that's the kind of thing that has to be taken care of during working hours, between the players themselves and in cooperation with the management. There's no escaping the fact that most top teams have a number of powerful personalities, fascinating types you can't avoid liking. Sometimes their actions or words make you wonder, but you have to reach some sort of compromise in your mind because you're probably going to be together for a long time, and you have to work well under intense circumstances.

All the travelling, the emotional climaxes, the fact that everybody knows exactly what mistakes have been made and what the consequences were, makes playing elite football a delicately balanced affair. To maintain a healthy working environment, it requires aggression, discretion, empathy and an enhanced understanding of the feelings of each of your colleagues. Over the last few years I've got to know the members of the present United squad pretty well because we've been through an awful lot together. Of course, what follows can't be a complete catalogue of all the players I've played alongside. So I have chosen to describe some of the main characters from our fabulous Treble season.

The star in the ascendant in the current United team is definitely Dwight Yorke, a sociable personality who in the relatively short time he has been at United has made a considerable impact, simply because of his buoyancy and optimism. Of course, he also plays a great game of football. He has greatly improved the atmosphere and United's overall game since his arrival from Aston Villa.

His most characteristic asset is his broad white smile, always evident regardless of how things are going. If he misses an obvious opportunity, he smiles; if he cocks up a penalty, he smiles; if he scores a goal, he smiles. He's also totally changed our changing room. You can always hear him and he constantly infects us with his positive vibes. The same applies to training, which was never such fun before Yorke joined the club.

The fact that he also delivers the goods on the field, where he has really clicked with Andy Cole, makes things even better. It's good to think that there probably isn't a single major club in Europe that doesn't now practise the dummy jump-over trick which Yorke and Cole have demonstrated so uniquely during our matches. The reality is, though, that the guys have never practised it. It simply came into being naturally as a result of a shared understanding of the game, intuitively emerging from the infinite number of possibilities presented by the heat of the action. Now it'll probably command a chapter of its own in coaching manuals.

When speaking about Yorke it's very difficult to avoid

talking about Andy Cole, who, in terms of personality, is the exact opposite. Cole is extremely sensitive, but a person I liked enormously from the moment I met him. He has always taken things very personally, even though he's tried to hide it and show a brave face. But he's also the kind of person you really want to encourage. For example, when he wasn't picked for the England squad, he always said, 'Actually I don't think I really wanted to be selected. The newspapers are unbearable. Look what they write!' I would say to him, 'It makes no difference what they write or say. What you've got to measure yourself by is what you do for our team. That's what counts. And here you're irreplaceable. You're our man.' That's how our conversations used to go. But now he's so much stronger; practically anything glances off him. Yorke's arrival at the club has strengthened Cole, no doubt about it. It hasn't made a new man of him – and thank goodness for that – but it has changed him noticeably. He's not so vulnerable, more extrovert, though not in Yorke's boisterous (and charming) way. You can really sense the difference. It's one good example of the marked changes Yorke's transfer to United has brought about.

Both of them are goalscorers, and you often hear of internal jealousies at other clubs, but that feeling simply didn't exist at United. We didn't care who scored the goals. The pleasure was shared, without any ulterior motives and without envy; any cockiness or excessive pride would have been slapped down immediately. To a man like Cole it makes no odds who scores, as long as it happens. He has won at Wembley; he has won the Premier League several times; he knows the value of collective strength, just like the rest of the team. And the funny thing – or at least the most remarkable – is that if you study their goals it becomes obvious how those two have specialised in delivering the ball to each other's feet. This makes them tremendously dangerous, a fact which European football has already noticed. It'll probably continue for many years to come, I should imagine.

This ethos of doing what is best for the club, not for yourself, is something Cole embraced long ago, and it has been interesting to observe his reactions to Alex Ferguson's substitutions, which usually bear fruit. Cole almost used to shake his head if Ferguson, for example, chose to start with Teddy Sheringham and Ole Gunnar Solskjaer up front. Not any more

But I'd like to change tack here and tell you a story. Again, Dwight Yorke is centre-stage – for once, though, in a role that didn't suit him at all. In fact, he later said that the incident rated among the most awful in his entire life.

The day before every weekend game, we had a recurrent joke which involved 'playing for the yellow jersey'. 'I've had a pally' was our expression for having had a bum day at training (the term referred to my old friend Gary Pallister, who quite frequently didn't exactly shine during training). The yellow jersey, or the 'pally', was given to whoever had fared worst at training. One fine day it was Yorke's turn to have it, in the judgement of Brian Kidd and Alex Ferguson, who functioned as referees during the ball-training at the end of the session.

Yorke was utterly gobsmacked. He launched into a vehement defence of himself, pointing out successful tackles he'd made and other unique things he'd managed during the session. My immediate reaction was that, in his usual jovial fashion, he was taking the piss, and he got as good as he gave until I spoke to him later in the showers. I still wasn't sure whether he was serious or pulling my leg when he said that it had been the worst day of his life, and that he had almost started crying when he was presented with the shirt. The incident had taken its toll on him, but his suffering wasn't over yet.

Later that day we were on our way to Sheffield to play Wednesday. Yorke was fined £500 because he had, it was presumed, dangerously overtaken Alex Ferguson on the way. It later transpired that it wasn't Yorke who had committed the offence but some other person driving the same kind of car!

But the damage had already been done. We lost 3–1 to Sheffield Wednesday the following day, and I'm convinced it was no coincidence. My opinion was shared by others, and it resulted in the consensus that it probably wasn't such a good idea for Yorke to be given the 'pally' again in future. He's never had it since. The system was changed so that instead of Brian Kidd and Alex Ferguson being the judges, every player on the winning team got a vote. After the result at Hillsborough, I don't think anyone had the nerve to vote for Dwight.

The Neville brothers were probably the two players on the team who gave me the most laughs. Both of them were, and are, incredibly serious about their football, though. Phil was always the only one who arrived at training at the same time as I did, about an hour before all the others. In a most un-English way, he warmed up with a series of exercises, and warmed down with loads of stretches after training. Quite unusual, but characteristic of the serious attitude which has supported his talent throughout his career so far.

For his big brother, Gary, things were perhaps a bit different. It was generally acknowledged at the club, and he even drew attention to it himself, that he was probably the one among the young generation at United who had the least natural talent of all. He grew up at the club together with such great talents as Giggs, Beckham and others, and my theory is that in compensation for his relative lack of skill he took on the role of the team's general organiser, a role that has stuck. He is almost in charge of the team. He keeps tabs on the various groups and all sorts of arrangements for his team-mates, and you can be sure that if Gary's involved everything will go smoothly, right down to the last detail. I have no reservations about predicting a great future for him at the club. In fact, I see him as a potential future captain at United, if not England. He has all the necessary qualities.

Gary may not be a natural, but he has developed, through sheer willpower, into a really good player with the kind of influence on the club spectators might not easily grasp. His favourite place on the field is undoubtedly right-back, although increasingly he's being given tasks in central defence, which he executes brilliantly. From his position at right-back he enjoys an enormously effective partnership with David Beckham. The two of them have an incredibly instinctive feeling and understanding of distribution on the right wing, something that is becoming more and more significant at United. Gary is a vociferous player who directs Beckham into position, ensuring the kind of fluent play that often results in a lethal Beckham cross into the box. To my mind, Gary's deployment on the right wing is the best way to exploit Beckham's obvious talent, and Beckham is never better than when he's playing with Gary Neville. (The two guys are best friends. Gary was David's best man at his wedding.) A final argument in favour of having Gary on the right flank is that his is probably one of the best throw-ins in the world. I certainly haven't seen any better, and we often scored goals from his touch-line delivery.

If I were asked to identify the perfect career at Manchester United I would have no hesitation. Of all the players on the team, the Welsh magician Ryan Giggs fits the bill. We started at United in the same year, 1991. Giggs was only seventeen then, a true star in the making who came into a team that needed just a few finishing touches to make it to the top. The following year we were champions, and from that day Giggs has been the mainstay of the best English team of the nineties.

We're talking about a world-class football star here, one who has managed to keep both feet firmly on the ground. With the help of his agent Harry Swales, he has steered his career clear of the temptations that always lie in wait for a guy of his calibre. He's a good-looking bloke, with huge appeal for the opposite sex, and he's been approached by a number of famous women. He's an amiable guy, congenial and witty, but even so he's managed to ensure that when people write or talk about Ryan Giggs they concentrate on football, with very few exceptions. Throughout his career, Ryan has been the best possible ambassador for the high standards associated with Manchester United. He is modest, rather shy in fact, and a thoroughly nice man.

For the football world it is, of course, a tragedy that Giggs plays for Wales – unless, that is, Wales manages at some time or other to qualify for the final stages of a major competition. He is a player who would be well suited to a European or World Cup finals, where I am sure he would raise his game.

David Beckham, another shining young star at United, has

automatically – especially because of his marriage to Spice Girl Victoria Adams – chosen a career path that's constantly in the limelight. They are the paparazzi's favourite victims, which means that they live under enormous pressure. Fortunately, it looks as though David can handle it, and I'm actually pretty impressed with the way he deals with all the hype that surrounds him. He's not knocked off balance easily, mainly because of his calm nature. He's amiable and extremely considerate, not the sort who likes to flex his muscles.

This state of harmony has been particularly useful to him during the 1998/99 season, which started with the uproar following his dismissal during the World Cup defeat against Argentina. It seemed he had to bear the blame for England's defeat alone. The result has been a torrent of verbal abuse at away matches. Songs have been sung about Victoria that are so disgusting it's incredible.

Even so, the 1998/99 season was Beckham's best ever, which is pretty impressive. It's a question of physical and mental strength, and Beckham's got both in abundance. He has the potential to become one of the greatest United players of all time.

The United midfield is also patrolled by two young players, Paul Scholes and Nicky Butt, both outstanding examples of the club's youth policy. Coaches Eric Harrison and Brian Kidd have influenced them very successfully and put just the right kind of motivation into their heads. Scholes is a meek and quiet young man, with a warm yet sharp wit. His comments are frequently so well-timed and succinct that you really have to have your wits about you to pick up the finer points. On the field, though, he's extremely serious. He has, perhaps, the best shot on the team, even though he's got quite small feet. Despite his modest size he's as strong as an ox and could run through a wall if necessary. Ideally he ought to play 'in the hole', but United don't generally play that way, so he shares orthodox midfield duties with Butt, Roy Keane and Ronny Johnsen.

In England it's absolutely vital to have top-class cover in every position. You can quickly run into a series of injuries and just as easily rack up a number of suspensions during a long and arduous season.

The captain and linchpin of United is, of course, Roy Keane. In my opinion, Keane is British football's greatest midfield player. He's incredibly vociferous and aggressive; his almost superhuman willpower makes him enormously valuable to the team. Earlier on in his career he sustained a really serious knee injury, an injury that only allows many players to get back perhaps 80 per cent joint mobility. Not Roy Keane. He changed as a player after the injury. He began to direct and distribute brilliantly, and was invariably in the right place at the right time. He is incredibly dangerous when he appears with a late run into the box, a skill he demonstrated perfectly towards the beginning of the 1999/2000 season with both the goals that secured a pulsating victory at Highbury. As a result of his injury, Roy has had to regrettably cut back on these incisive breaks, but he can still be devastating. Now he has become more of a controller. He has taken on a new role, one he fulfils fully to this day – when he's not getting into trouble, that is. He has a fiery Irish temper.

Then there's Ole Gunnar Solskjaer, the icy cool Norwegian. It's sickening to have a player of his quality sitting on the bench. He doesn't get as much time on the field as Cole and Yorke, but in my opinion he's the best front-runner on the United team. He's purely and simply the thinker among our strikers, an extremely calculating footballer who's highly aware of everything he does. He has incredible powers of perception and senses the potential a situation has to offer in a flash. Somehow he knows exactly what the goalkeeper is thinking and reacts accordingly. That's why some of his goals look a bit unorthodox. The fact that he's extremely positive and always in good spirits is another huge bonus for United. His only problem is, of course, that he often starts a match on the bench, but I have a feeling he accepts this role. I also know that Alex Ferguson is very careful to ensure that Ole Gunnar gets to play enough. United don't want to lose him.

Teddy Sheringham can seem a bit arrogant at first sight, and I must admit this was my impression of him when he was my opponent. But I've since discovered this isn't the case. In fact he's a bit shy and basically quite unsure of himself at times. He's an extremely valuable player who has in many respects been able to fill the gap left by Eric Cantona. He has something of the same understanding of the game; in particular he has an incredible eye for playing long through-balls. He can also hold the ball up well. He was an excellent buy, and he's a good man with it.

So I've talked about some of my fellow players here; many more could have been mentioned, all of them good colleagues but, as I said before, few of them close friends. Such is life!

13 The Press

'I trust people – at least until convinced otherwise. I expect others to show me some respect at least, and am disappointed when they don't. Since I'm not exactly the kind of person to hold himself back when provoked, I often react without thinking. This has obviously been instrumental in giving me a reputation of being quick-tempered and quite difficult to deal with. I believe I have a right to be like that, and personally I can live with it – even though it means that I don't have to step far out of line before I draw flak in the press. Such is life.'

W HILE I HAVE BEEN WRITING this autobiography, I've found it necessary to look into every corner of my life in order to paint as full a picture as possible. For me, contact with the media has always played a fundamental part in my life.

Generally speaking, I have an excellent relationship with the press, both in England and in Denmark. As yet, I don't have any relationship with the Portuguese press, but that's probably just a matter of time.

As in all other aspects of life, you rarely remember the good things in detail. The reverse side of the coin is that you can vividly recall episodes which have hurt you deeply. This chapter will deal with a couple of incidents which have hurt my family and me. Hopefully, it will also serve to illustrate how things can be twisted by the media to achieve the desired fit. It's not my intention to seek revenge against certain elements of the media; rather, I wish to give people an understanding of the fact that not everything they read is the gospel truth.

To deal with the press as I and others do, it takes acute awareness. You have to take great care with your choice of words. And you need to communicate an agenda of your own. It can be done . . . most of the time.

I have been on the receiving end, too. To this day, newspaper articles concerning me can be misleading. What I actually say to a reporter can be ignored or twisted in the name of a good story.

My career was in its infancy when I got, if not my first shock, then my first insight into the ways of journalists. I made my debut in the First Division with Hvidovre. We were to play Esbjerg, who had a guy called Ole Kjaer between the posts. The match went pretty well for me, and the following day I was able to read, for the first time, praise of my work in the press. A few days later the local paper wanted to interview me. No problem.

We talked for a long time. I was young. I was starting out on what I hoped would be a long and successful career. I talked nineteen to the dozen about football, especially about being a goalkeeper. I talked about Dino Zoff and Peter Shilton, and said that my ambition was to reach their level of performance since – in my opinion – Denmark had never had a goalkeeper in that category. We are talking about the world's two best goalkeepers of all time! So I was flabbergasted when I saw the paper and its headline, QVIST AND KJAER HOPELESS, which hardly represented my opinion of two of Denmarks's best goalkeepers at the time. (Ole Qvist was the Danish national goalkeeper.)

But for the tabloid *Ekstra Bladet*, it was right up their street, and the next day they condensed the article and attributed to me the following tender words about my colleagues: 'I'm not afraid to say that if I can't be better than Ole Qvist and Ole Kjaer then I'm not good enough for the Denmark squad.' Quite a statement, and one that didn't exactly make my life easier. It also left its mark, especially on my relationship with Ole Qvist.

I shared a few national team training sessions with Qvist, and it would be no exaggeration to call our relationship strained. The situation annoyed me tremendously because Qvist could have been an invaluable mentor to me at that stage of my career. But I was still a bit green and didn't really know how to handle the situation. So nothing happened, until one day when an opportunity to put matters right arose. It was at journalist Jorgen Herbert's fortieth birthday party. At some stage, Big Werner – who really liked me despite the fact that he was the biggest KB fan ever – came over to me and said: 'Now's your chance to clear the air between you and Ole Qvist. He's standing right over there. Go on!' I walked over to him.

It turned out that the situation was rather getting to him. He explained how he had felt pretty disappointed in me and couldn't really understand how a young lad who hadn't even played an international match yet could have made a statement like that. I told him how much I regretted what had happened and explained that the story was the result of a certain amount of journalistic licence. I don't know if he ever accepted my apology because I've never met him since, but I was certainly pleased to have got the matter off my chest, and I'm still glad I did it.

This little episode taught me some important points. You've got to watch your mouth when talking to reporters, and at the same time you've got to realise there are all kinds of people out there reading these stories, some of whom can get hurt if they are innocently drawn into the content of the interview as the journalist presents it.

When Manchester United were playing an away game in the Champions' League, we usually left the day before the game. We would meet at Manchester airport at eight o'clock in the morning and would always be met by the entire press, waiting for comments from coaches and players. Before the Borrusia Dormund semi-final in 1997, three tabloid newspapers asked me to compare the present team with that of 1968. I said that such a comparison was impossible because it could only be based on speculation. I also said that most world-class club teams today would be able to beat the 1968 team 10–0 because the physical, technical and tactical aspects of the game have changed enormously over the last 30 years. But I stressed that this wasn't meant as an attack on the great team, a team that I have the greatest respect for, but merely an illustration of the extent to which the game has moved on. In addition, I stressed to the journalists that I didn't wanted my comments to make the headlines. If they did, I would cease to collaborate with them.

The next day the 'story' was splashed across the sports pages of the three newspapers concerned. It was the story of the day; the headlines were huge. As you would expect, the journalists had talked to some of the players from the 1968 team about Schmeichel's 'attack' on them. The whole thing ended in tears. When I met the reporters in question after the game, I headed straight for them. All the important figures in the media pack were there and the TV cameras were rolling. The journalists excused themselves by claiming that their stories had been cut and twisted by the office staff. They placed all the blame squarely at the door of their editors. This is a well known phenomenon. It is never the reporter you talk to who is responsible but always the editor back in London or Copenhagen. The fact of the matter was that they had got their story, sold their newspapers, and didn't give me a moment's thought.

But the papers use us to sell their product, and in return they give you an opportunity to publish your thoughts if you've got something on your mind. These are the terms of the media industry to which at least some Danish newspapers subscribe, and when it's done honourably it's not a problem. The reporters put more or less intelligent questions to you and you try to answer as best you can and hope to be quoted more or less accurately. Fortunately, the relationship between reporters and their sources is by and large pretty good, based on the knowledge that our paths will continue to cross, that we all have a job to do, and we have to stand the sight of each other tomorrow as well.

I've had many fine experiences with highly professional journalists of solid integrity. One of the best interviews I ever did was with Ninka (a pseudonym) of *Politiken*, a respected daily newspaper. She could hardly claim to have the greatest knowledge of football. Her working methods, on the other hand, impressed me. When she came to my house in England, she proved herself a journalist who was prepared to the fingertips. She knew absolutely everything there was to know about my career, and I had the feeling that she already knew the answers to all her questions. This situation made me feel very relaxed and gave me the freedom to talk about numerous topics of interest to me, about which I didn't usually express an opinion. When I read the finished article I was even more impressed. It was a smashing portrait, and nothing had been taken out of context. Not one quote was wrong. It was a pleasure to read.

Fortunately, there are also many top-notch professional sports reporters. I consider many of them good acquaintances with whom I can discuss subjects of common interest without the fear of being exploited. I often speak to first-rate reporters such as Steen Ankerdal of *Berlingske Tidende*, Soren Olsen of *Politiken* and several of *Jyllands-Posten*'s people. These conversations don't always result in an article, but they're always interesting, and occasionally the odd snippet crops up in another article. Men like Peter Gronborg of *Politiken* and Peter Phil from DR's sports radio are reporters with considerable clout. Trustworthy and knowledgeable, they have a thorough insight into the finer points of the sporting world.

But still there are some individuals who you can't trust. Not many, but they are there. These journalists quote people in accordance with the story they wish to tell. They are not concerned in the least about the consequences for the involved parties.

Once something has been aired, it's already a story in itself. When Denmark played Wales in Liverpool in June 1999, Tommy Poulsen from the Danish paper *Horsens Folkeblad* wrote that Flemming Serritslev would become the new national coach. This information he plucked from thin air. Yet once it appears in print, and the story has hit the news stands, it is pretty much considered a reality. I had been kept informed all the way through the selection process and I knew exactly at what stage the Danish FA had reached in their deliberations. At this point, those responsible weren't even close to appointing Serritslev. But one reporter had seen it differently, filed the story accordingly, and all the other newspapers followed suit.

It's rather like a political scandal. A politician necessarily has to talk to the press: it's an absolutely central part of his role. If a bad-tempered journalist has it in for him, a political scandal can be created at the drop of a hat, simply my misquoting the politician. Of course, he can always claim that he had not been quoted correctly but, in turn, this can be interpreted simply as an attempt to wriggle out of trouble.

My words have frequently been subjected to such

distortion, and the most distressing thing about the situation is that you feel completely defenceless. Of course you can complain, as I did to *Ekstra Bladet* in the spring of 1999, but going down this road can lead only to more despair, and I'd like to illustrate that point with the exchange of letters that took place between my lawyer and *Ekstra Bladet*. Not because the letters have much to do with football, but because the business both fascinates and appals me. The letters that follow are I think a good example of how a newspaper can shun its responsibility to the truth and then weave a grotesque web of poor excuses, attempting to explain things away with a cockiness I find out of place when such serious matters are being considered.

Since the reason why the letters were written is made clear by the letters themselves, I shall go straight on to the first one my lawyer sent to *Ekstra Bladet*:

Ekstra Bladet
Copenhagen

Attn: The Editor in Chief, Bent Falbert/reporters Jan Jensen and Finn Stilling

20 April 1999

As Peter Schmeichel's lawyer, I am writing to you in connection with the exclusive interview published in *Ekstra Bladet* on Saturday, 17 April 1999. The article was written after reporters Jan Jensen and Finn Stilling visited Peter Schmeichel and in a friendly atmosphere spent quite some time discussing Peter Schmeichel's past, as well as his future plans.

The article itself contains numerous errors and erroneous information. It can naturally make one wonder how two reporters can misunderstand so much in such a short time as they did in their conversation with Peter Schmeichel. However, Peter Schmeichel has no intention of taking further action on this count.

The interview with Peter Schmeichel was presented in grand style in *Ekstra Bladet*, both on newsagents' poster boards and on the front page on 17 April 1999. On the poster board was a large picture of Peter Schmeichel with the headline 'You are malicious'. This is repeated on section 2 and on the front page of section 1 is a picture of Peter Schmeichel with reference to the exclusive interview. Beside the picture is the following text: 'The Danes are malicious'. On pages 10 and 11 of section 2 an extremely prominent headline announces: 'The malicious Danes'. Throughout, the headlines are: 'You are malicious', 'The Danes are malicious' and 'The malicious Danes'.

The interview, which, as mentioned previously, took place in a positive and friendly atmosphere, provides no basis whatsoever to support these headlines. Peter Schmeichel has said nothing whatsoever which the reporters present could have construed as meaning that he generally considers the Danes to be malicious.

The headlines are, therefore, entirely unacceptable and I must on behalf of Peter Schmeichel demand that *Ekstra Bladet* apologises to Peter Schmeichel, in a manner clear and unambiguous to its readers, for having used these headlines which, although the headlines apparently applied to the Danes, are insulting to Peter Schmeichel. He would never dream of making such statements.

I must therefore demand that *Ekstra Bladet*, using equally prominent headlines on both poster boards and the front page of *Ekstra Bladet*, announces that *Ekstra Bladet*'s two reporters have thoroughly misunderstood Peter Schmeichel, or that those who are responsible for the layout of the poster boards, front pages and headlines have either not read the article or have entirely and unjustifiably attempted, out of desire to create a sensation, to produce a headline for which there was no basis in the interview itself.

If such an apology does not appear within seven days, I have been instructed by Peter Schmeichel to consider the possibility of legal action against *Ekstra Bladet* in order to establish that the headlines on the poster boards, the front pages and in the article itself are not the statements of Peter Schmeichel, and that *Ekstra Bladet* was in no way entitled to quote him for the statements.

Peter Schmeichel has in addition asked me to inform you that he in future does not wish to have further contact with *Ekstra Bladet*'s reporters.

I look forward to your immediate reply.

Yours sincerely,

K.L. Nemeth

Ekstra Bladet had asked me whether I would be returning to Brondby after leaving United. My answer was that I didn't see myself going back because it didn't seem like the right thing to do. Many players who had returned to Denmark after a spell abroad had advised me against going back. Just as importantly, I didn't think it would be right for the children. In my home country they would never be anything other than 'Peter Schmeichel's kids' and they would be somehow held responsible for my performanes on the football field. I gave the reporters an example of how kids treat each other from time to time. Kasper had been off somewhere playing football and a couple of children teased him about something that I had done during a match. I told the journalists that children can be malicious towards each other. Hardly the same thing as claiming that all Danes are malicious!

After the letter was sent, two days elapsed, during which *Ekstra Bladet* chewed over the complaint. Of course they had no intention of complying with my demands. Doing so would never occur to them, as can clearly be seen from the fax below which streamed out of my machine on 22 April. The same day my lawyer received a letter from Bent Falbert who said he had already 'had an article inserted in *Ekstra Bladet* in which you will be able to voice your opinion.' I will return to this article. But first the fax from Bent Falbert:

Dear Peter Schmeichel,

I understand from a letter by your lawyer Karoly Nemeth dated 20 April that you are dissatisfied with the headlines in the interview with you which we printed last Saturday.

Chief sports reporter Jan Jensen tells me that he had a conversation with you last weekend which he followed up with a fax in which he offered you the chance to explain your point of view. On the basis of this it seems rather excessive for you to have gone running to a lawyer.

So as to accommodate your criticism I have printed an article in the Thursday edition of *Ekstra Bladet* in which you have the opportunity to make your views known. According to your lawyer's letter you were satisfied with the content of the interview itself. It was the headlines alone that worried you. However, the reporters say there was ample basis for the headlines in what you said in the interview.

I understand from the reporters that it was on your own initiative that you aired misgivings about returning to your old country when your football career is over. It can hardly come as a surprise to you that this element of the interview was used in the headline, since it constituted the most obviously newsworthy element of the conversation.

I take it that Thursday's article will clear the air. It would be an awful mess if Denmark's great goalkeeper and Denmark's great newspaper were to be on bad terms with each other.

Yours sincerely,
Bent Falbert

I sat for ages gaping at this fax, which I considered to be a masterpiece of hollow, smarmy, irrelevant nonsense. I thought it interesting that despite the fact that my lawyer wrote in his first letter 'the article itself contains numerous errors and erroneous information', Bent Falbert concluded that I was 'satisfied with the content of the interview itself'. Like hell I was. I had counted no fewer than sixteen factual errors, which came as no surprise considering that I don't recall Jan Jensen writing a single note during our three-hour conversation or Finn Stilling scribbling down anything more than the odd significant word or two. But there was nothing to be done about the factual errors; I was hoping to get *Ekstra Bladet* to retract its liberal interpretation of the interview, of which the headlines were just an expression.

That hope diminished as I sat there with the fax, and disappeared altogether when later that day I read the letter

Bent Falbert had sent to my lawyer. This one didn't seem to me so smarmy; instead I thought it adopted an aggressive, harsh tone:

Dear Karoly Nemeth,

Re. *Ekstra Bladet*'s interview with Peter Schmeichel, 17 April 1999

In your fax of 20 April you complain about the headlines of the above interview. You also indicate that Peter Schmeichel's account in the interview itself is okay.

It is amazing that you make it sound as though you know what Schmeichel said to two of our most experienced sports reporters during a conversation in England at which you were not present.

According to Jan Jensen and Finn Stilling, Peter Schmeichel himself broached the subject of his having misgivings about returning to Denmark at the end of his football career because he found that many Danes were malicious and that envy was rife. This evaluation came as a surprise to the reporters but was the most sensational aspect of the three-hour-long interview. For that reason this theme naturally ended up in the headlines.

As far as I can see, Schmeichel's objection is purely that he interprets the headlines as though we make him accuse every single Dane of being malicious. He probably only means that many of them are. We do not believe that we have suggested anything other than what was acknowledged by Schmeichel.

But since it is pointless for Denmark's great goalkeeper and its great newspaper to be at odds with each other for such petty reasons, I have published an article in the Thursday edition making known Schmeichel's misgivings about how he was launched on to the front page. Schmeichel had already complained to chief sports reporter Jan Jensen in a conversation last weekend. Following this, Jan Jensen offered him in a fax the opportunity to express his views about *Ekstra Bladet*'s headlines in as many words as he liked. Instead he chose to involve you, which to me appears rather unnecessary.

In any case I think we have now got things straight and I consider the case to be closed.

Yours sincerely,

Bent Falbert

This letter was also pretty hard to beat, and it in no way accommodated me or my demands. All the same, it was impressive to see how Bent Falbert, I felt, almost tied his tongue in knots trying to find a way out of the problem. One sentence in particular was, I believe, a masterpiece of word-twisting: 'As far as I can see, Schmeichel's objection is purely that he interprets the headlines as though we make him accuse every single Dane of being malicious.' For me it wasn't a question of 'interpreting' the headlines; what other way is their of interpreting 'You are malicious', 'The Danes are malicious' or 'The malicious Danes'?

A reference is made to a telephone conversation between Jan Jensen and myself. It took place the day after the article had appeared in the paper. During our hour-long discussion, I took Jensen through every single inaccuracy. I ended up asking him whether he thought I had used the words 'Danes' and 'malicious' in that context. He finally admitted that I hadn't. He didn't apologise, and he probably never will.

Unfortunately, their problem became my problem, and the so-called 'article' in which I was supposed to tell my side of the story bore the headline SCHMEICHEL: NOT ALL DANES ARE MALICIOUS. After this I realised there was nothing I could do. The paper reserves the right freely to interpret what people say, me included. I couldn't be bothered to have any part of it in future, so I got my lawyer to bring the case to a close with the following letter:

3 May 1999

Dear Bent Falbert,

Re.: Peter Schmeichel

Thank you for your reply of 22 April 1999 – if one can call it a reply, that is. I would be more inclined to call it a load of twaddle. Let us agree that Peter is, after all, the one who knows best what he said and the way he said it.

In your letter you mention Denmark's great goalkeeper and Denmark's 'great newspaper'. What newspaper is that you are referring to? Is it the one that yet again has demonstrated its lack of ethics and seriousness as recently as 23 April 1999 by finding, despite Peter's protest, yet another opportunity to publish that incorrect and perfidious headline?

The so-called 'disclaimer' is *Ekstra Bladet*'s usual form of disclaimer and, if this is possible, is even more erroneous than the article which *Ekstra Bladet* published in the first place.

May I inform you, on behalf of Denmark's great goalkeeper, that Peter Schmeichel no longer wants any contact with *Ekstra Bladet*, and any approach made by reporters from *Ekstra Bladet* will either be ignored or rejected.
Yours sincerely,
K. L. Nemeth

Family and friends suffer greatly when something like this happens. But the ones that suffer the most in the end are, of course, the readers of the newspapers. They are taken for a ride by journalists and editors who don't give a damn so long as the paper gets out.

Naturally, Bente and I went to the wedding of Victoria Adams and David Beckham. The whole team was invited. Since the wedding was probably the media event of the summer, it caused ripples in the Danish press too. Bente wasn't particularly comfortable about this. She is the kind of person who would much rather be out of the limelight. So it hurt her deeply that a reporter from *Ekstra Bladet*, Trine Villemann – a rather charmless women, in my opinion – described Bente's dress as something you would put presents under at Christmas. I will resist the temptation to comment on Trine Villemann's own appearance, but she should not make comments about other people's.

Bente has never done anything to hurt anybody. She certainly didn't deserve that kind of unforgivable treatment.

Another example of the press inventing a story concerns my so-called 'farewell party' at Restaurant Etcetera in Copenhagen in July 1999. At one point during my summer holiday I had dined there and got into conversation with the manager. He had heard that I played the drums and thought that a little jam session might be fun. He suggested it take place in the restaurant on a quiet day. The plan was to play ten numbers on a Tuesday night. I invited my parents, a couple of friends and, of course, Bente, Cecilie and Kasper so that they could enjoy my debut as a musician! The evening was to be no more than that.

The restaurant is quite a trendy place to eat and the press' interpretation of the event was that I threw a goodbye party for all my jet-set friends. A number of people whom I only know by name were identified as my close friends in newspaper reports. Jesper Skibby, a famous Danish professional cyclist, was mentioned but he wasn't even there. Another cyclist, Brian Holm, certainly was there but how can you expect journalists to know the difference?

I was there to play the drums. Nothing else. Sometimes I have great trouble recognising the world in which journalists live.

But I sense that readers are becoming less and less interested in this kind or journalism. Both *Ekstra Bladet* and *BT* have flagging circulation figures. I take this as a sign that things are changing. TV and radio stations are faster with the news than newspapers, but they are all trailing behind the internet, and it's my guess that here lies the future of news media. I'm in the process of developing my own homepage because I firmly believe the internet is the future of communication. I'm determined to get involved – luckily, this new technology really interests me – and it will undoubtedly save me considerable time if in the future I'll be able to communicate directly via the homepage instead of talking to dozens of reporters every day.

There is light at the end of the tunnel, after all.

14 World Cup 1998

'I still love playing football, and I enjoy my life, but sometimes press conferences are just too much! There were journalists from all over the world at the meeting today, but to be asked the same stupid questions about the Saudi Arabian goalkeeper, about whether I still talk to Cantona, about the new guidelines for referees and all kinds of other drivel, that was just a bit more than I could take today.'

I SPENT THE WORLD CUP in France playing football and working for the media. Danish TV2 had asked me to do some interviews for them, and I also kept a daily diary, mainly for my own benefit. When I read it through after the tournament had finished, it seemed to me that the diary not only provided a good overview of those testing days in the Danish camp, but it also reflected my feelings about life in places like the south of France, which played a role in my decision to leave Manchester United. My experiences in France seemed to me to represent something of a personal watershed, so I've chosen to reproduce my diary here, even though it contains a number of critical comments. But that's the way I felt at the time.

Sunday, 7 June

The World Cup starts today – or, to be more precise, we leave for France today. I arrived at the airport at 9.30 this morning with Bente and the children. They'd been given a special pass so that they could join me in the airport building. The DBU [Danish Football Association] had invited us all to breakfast at the Tivoli Inn in Copenhagen, and it turned out to be very pleasant.

Farewell scenes are strange things. Cecilie was in tears at the prospect of being separated from her dad for such a long time. She looks so sweet when she cries! Kasper, on the other hand, was very cool, but I think he just puts up with it. They were also leaving by plane for Manchester at 4.25 this afternoon. They have to go to school tomorrow.

We were booked to fly economy class, which didn't really surprise me. But it did strike me how stingy the DBU are. The players' efforts result in a million-pound-plus turnover but the DBU are still so bloody tight-fisted! The flight itself was fine, although we did bump around in some turbulence. It took two and a half hours, followed by another two hours by bus! Again, I can't help wondering about the DBU's miserly attitude, because it wouldn't have been any problem to charter a plane to Marseilles, which is only 40 kilometres from St Cyr sur Mer, where the Danish squad is staying.

It's a really lovely hotel. Not luxurious, but it's set in a beautiful landscape with a golf course and a view looking straight out on to the Mediterranean. From my room I have an unobstructed view of the eighteenth green. When we arrived there was a table waiting for us in reception with a spread of the most delicious sticks of French bread, about three feet in length – just what we needed since we hadn't had anything to eat or drink since ten o'clock this morning.

Just before we arrived at the hotel, we made a little detour to visit the town square, where we were received by the mayor and some of the local residents. They seem to be very proud to have us staying here.

After taking a little nap, we went for a training session at a stadium in Toulon, a twenty-minute drive from the hotel. A lovely little ground with a good pitch. As usual, we had the press around us for the first quarter of an hour. But that was soon over because they were only interested in the injury I had sustained last Friday in the friendly against Cameroon. And that's all right now. The most stupid question had already been asked this morning, when we were boarding the plane. A journalist from Danish Radio TV-News, who is always particularly arrogant, asked me: 'How many times do you think you'll have to fish the ball out of the back of the net in France?' I just told him that I thought it was a really silly question, turned round and boarded the plane.

After we'd eaten our evening meal, I met Gebhart Reusch,

my friendly German glove sponsor. We'd originally agreed to meet tomorrow, but Germans often drive very fast, so he'd arrived a bit earlier than planned. He was in France with his South American agent, whose name I don't remember. But it was nice meeting Gebhart again. As he's staying at the hotel tonight, I've arranged to have breakfast with him in the morning.

Monday, 8 June

We have now been at the Hotel de Fregate at St Cyr sur Mer in Bandol for 24 hours and we're starting to feel at home. After the unnecessarily wearing trip yesterday, it was difficult to get out of bed this morning, but I finally managed it.

I said goodbye to Gebhart Reusch and his Argentinian friend, and went off for another training session in Toulon. The press were there again. I had a chat with Jakob Kjeldberg, who told me that Danish TV3 had broadcast a live transmission of our training session yesterday. Get a life! Torben Larsen, from the Danish tabloid *BT*, tried to open up a story about pecking-orders in the national team, but to his surprise I objected in no uncertain terms. Asger, a cameraman from DR-Sport, had rung home to headquarters to find out who the clot was who had asked me that ridiculous question at the airport yesterday. He was told to give me an apology. It's a bit of a pity that the DR-Sport people working down here have to act as messengers and smooth things out, because they are in fact really nice individuals.

After lunch we finally got on to the golf course. My game was a bit like the course – up and down – but it was a fantastic round on the most dramatic golf course I have ever seen. I played with Marc Rieper, Jes Hogh and Toffe – Stig Tofting. Toffe is quite a good golfer – in his own special way. His style is aggressive but elegant, and very effective at the same time. He's also very impatient, which made me a bit nervous, and I think that affected by game a bit. Marc won the game, but he played well, so he deserved to. And the course was, as I said, a delight. Very imaginatively laid out with attractive bunkers, dramatic bunkers and bunkers that demand nerve and strength. It was also blowing a gale, which didn't make things any easier. We teed off at 1.30 and didn't finish until 6.30! I'll try to get up a bit earlier tomorrow so I can go over and practise on the driving range.

Martin Jorgensen kicked off our evening meeting by inviting us to take part in a dream-team competition, just like they have in *BT*. He said he would take care of all the practical arrangements. I don't think he realises how much work is involved, but he's also new in the squad.

I'm dead tired. I'm going to bed now!

Tuesday, 9 June

Today I bought a 'Big Bertha' driver to add to my set of golf clubs – or, to be more precise, the 'Biggest Bertha'. After having tried it out on the driving range I have to conclude that I slice like a maniac. I played 80 balls and hit about 60, of which 40 were sliced, and it was driving me mad! While I was standing there slicing, a school group returned from the course with their teacher, and they all stood there to watch Peter Schmeichel play! They wanted autographs and photos, but when I declined, explaining that I was training, the woman teacher told me that I was arrogant, which prompted me to call her a bitch. I'm not sure who came out on top in this exchange, but apparently there's nowhere where I can be allowed to be just Peter and work on my golfing technique.

During the afternoon I played with Jorgen Henriksen, and then we went on a very enjoyable stroll in the hills. I'm pretty sure that with a bit of practice I could become quite good at golf, because I swung my irons pretty well and managed to play a fairly good round. I almost know what I'm doing!

Kasper rang to tell me that he had won a fishing competition in Denmark and the prize would probably be a pair of waders. I was very pleased to hear this, but it irritates me that I can't be there with him. I'll make a real effort to go fishing with him when things quieten down a bit.

The World Cup officially kicks off tomorrow, and I thought

I'd be able to feel it in the atmosphere, but everybody is very relaxed and taking the situation calmly. I think playing golf helps a lot. The only person who perhaps seems a little tense is Bo Johansson, or 'Bosse' as he is known.

The training schedule keeps changing. Today we started at 10.30 and didn't finish until 12.20, but perhaps it will be shorter tomorrow. Maybe I read the signals wrongly, but something is different.

We have finally got our card club going, and it's a really good idea from my point of view. It turned out to be both a lucrative and an entertaining evening, even though some of the participants had stomach trouble!

Just in front of my window, next to the eighteenth green, there's a little lake with frogs. At night they croak like mad and make a hell of a noise. Suddenly they go quiet, then perhaps ten seconds go by until one of them starts again, and then they all join in. And that's how they carry on until they all become too tired to croak! I've only been told about this, because it usually happens about one o'clock in the morning and by that time I'm sleeping like a log. And that's what I'm going to do now!

Wednesday, 10 June

The World Cup games started today and that means it won't be long before it's time for our first match. Brazil beat Scotland 2–1, and Norway were lucky to draw 2–2 with Morocco. Norway played the crappiest game of football I've ever seen, which wouldn't irritate me so much if it wasn't for the fact that Drillo [the Norwegian national team coach at the time] knows so much about football! I hope they don't qualify for the second round, even though it will be a shame for Henning Berg, Ronnie Johnsen and Ole Gunnar, but they aren't responsible for the way the Norwegians play.

Yesterday the press were allowed to visit our hotel so that they could let the people in Denmark know where we're staying. All the newspapers have written good, sober stories about their visit apart from Steen Uno from *BT* who apparently felt cheated for some reason or another. That made him write the worst mud-slinging story in living memory. For example, he wrote that we wouldn't allow ourselves to be photographed bare-chested in swimming trunks, or 'undressed' as he put it, to which he added that we had been exposed enough anyway in our preparation games. The swine!

I've completed the first part of my diary for TV2. Flemming Toft came to pick me up at the hotel, and then we got on with recording my 'spots'. So far I haven't found it difficult speaking to camera, but I don't know how I'll react the day I'm left on my own without a 'babysitter'!

Kasper hasn't been to school today because he hurt his back yesterday. I don't think it's all that serious, and I think perhaps he's using it as a bit of an excuse to get some sympathy from his mother while he's at home with her.

We've been playing cards, and it's still extremely entertaining!

Early tomorrow morning we leave for Lens, and that's the real start of our World Cup. It'll be great, because even though it's fun to train and enjoy the build-up, it's much better to make a start and play some games.

Today police in Denmark arrested a 50-year-old man for the murder of a little girl called Susan near where I used to play in Brondby. I hope that every day of the rest of his life will be hell for him, and that his fellow prisoners remind him regularly what a pig he is. Sometimes I'm ashamed of being a man. I've thought a lot about Susan's family today, about what they have already been through and what they will have to go through now that the little girl's murderer has been identified. They have my greatest sympathy, and I just wish that there was something I could do to ease their pain. But there's nothing I can do, and that is the most heartbreaking thing of all. If only it would never happen again!

Thursday, 11 June

What a day!

It's the day before we play our first game, and our programme has been a bit too tough. We left our hotel at 8.45

this morning for the airport at Marseilles. It's only a 40-minute drive, but our police escort managed to double that time. This was followed by a flight lasting an hour and three quarters, and finally a half-hour drive to the stadium where we're going to play tomorrow. We ate lunch there, and then there was a press conference!

I still love playing football, and I enjoy my life, but sometimes press conferences are just too much! There were journalists from all over the world at the meeting today, but to be asked the same stupid questions about the Saudi Arabian goalkeeper, about whether I still talk to Cantona, about the new guidelines for referees and all kinds of other drivel, that was just a bit more than I could take today. But we all have that kind of day!

If I think about the positives of the day, the pitch springs immediately to mind. It was like the surface of a billiards table, and, as it was pouring down with rain, it will undoubtedly be just right for the game.

To round off a really long day of travelling, we also had a one-hour journey to the hotel. But we did get to see a bit of TV. We saw the game between Italy and Chile, which ended in a 2–2 draw and was so boring that I fell asleep. However, it's possible my judgement was influenced by the fact that I was very tired after the day's exertions.

Our squad is in good shape the day before our first match. Everyone seems keyed up without being tense, and that's usually a good sign. We all appear to be looking forward to it. I certainly am. And as our game is at 5.30 tomorrow afternoon, I need all the rest I can get.

Friday, 12 June

We finally played our first game. And what a start we got off to! A 1–0 victory against Saudi Arabia. Three points in the bag! We couldn't have wished for a better start.

Right from the start of the day I could tell how geared up we all were. It wasn't that easy-going atmosphere which is characteristic of the squad, but a very healthy kind of nervousness. I was also nervous, but not because I was worried about playing. I was more worried about us not getting off to a good start.

The starting line-up was as follows: Peter Schmeichel, Soren Colding, Marc Rieper, Jes Hogh, Michael Schjonberg, Martin Jorgensen, Thomas Helveg, Morten Wieghorst, Michael Laudrup, Brian Laudrup and Ebbe Sand. It was Michael Laudrup's 100th international, and he played really well. Marc Rieper headed our goal halfway through the second half, following a perfect cross from Brian Laudrup. It's not often that Marc scores, but when he does they're almost always very important goals. We played all right, but there's definitely room for improvement.

After the game I tried in vain to get hold of Bente and the children, but there was no answer on the mobile or at home. We had arranged to ring each other, so I couldn't understand why her mobile wasn't turned on.

We ate a light meal at the airport. We were told the reason we couldn't fly to Marseilles straight away was that the plane was delayed. But I think there was another reason: France were playing South Africa that night. So we sat down at the airport and watched the game.

Saturday, 13 June

There's an incredible amount of optimism in the squad. We're all happy, and there's every reason for us to be so.

Then we saw excerpts of our game on Danish TV3, and I have to admit I was disappointed by the harsh judgements passed, by Preben Elkjaer in particular. He thought it a victory where we just did what was necessary against a side that had nothing to offer. He didn't think we'd played well at all; he said we'd lacked coordination and had very little rhythm. How quickly people forget, I thought to myself. Preben has played in the World Cup. He is aware of the pressures surrounding an opening match and he should know better than to slaughter us in that way. When Denmark beat Scotland 1–0 in Mexico, and Preben was playing, it was an excellent result. It was a very similar game to the one yesterday.

The Danish newspapers weren't really any better, but then they don't know a bloody thing! Especially not the new sports editor of *Ekstra Bladet*, Jan Jensen, who I reckon knows absolutely nothing. Unfortunately, we only receive three Danish newspapers every day: *Ekstra Bladet* and *BT*, and *Jyllands-Posten*, which thankfully is a good paper. I miss *Politiken* and 'Auntie' Berlinger [*Berlingske Tidende*] and I can't understand why we can't receive them down here.

Spain lost to Nigeria today, and that's very interesting because if we qualify for the second round we have to meet a team from their group. Spain were leading 2–1, but then Zubizaretta made a terrible mistake which unfortunately cost them the game.

I've been on the driving range again today, and I'm getting better with my three-iron. But if I'm going to improve I'll have to take some lessons. I think I'll do that because I've decided to take my golf more seriously. I really think I could work my way down to a ten handicap.

Sunday, 14 June

When I got off the bus I discovered I'd forgotten my boots. That cost me a 'fine' of £50, which went straight into our 'penalty box'. While my boots were being fetched, I borrowed a pair from Mogens Krogh, our reserve goalie, and even though we use the same kind of boots, his were – funnily enough – more comfortable to wear!

I played golf again for the rest of the day. I'm really getting addicted to it, and the better you get, the more you enjoy playing. I realised that today, when I played some of the best golf I've ever managed. Per Frandsen and I scored 33 stableford points, Rieper 28, while Stig scored so few it's not worth mentioning. Stig is still frustrating to play with. He's full of energy and very impatient, which can be very irritating when you're trying to concentrate. Apart from that, he's good fun to be on the course with because he's so positive and he plays golf in the most delightful way. He uses something that resembles a baseball grip when he holds a club, and even though it looks rather awkward, he really plays quite well.

I haven't seen much football today, because you can't be on the golf course and in front of a TV at the same time. This evening we played cards while Croatia were playing against Jamaica, and with their usual luck Croatia won 3–1. They shouldn't really have reached the finals: if we'd beaten them 4–1 instead of 3–1 in Copenhagen and lost 1–0 in Athens to Greece instead of drawing 0–0, Croatia would have finished in third place in our group.

Borge Tud [a small-time players' agent and hanger-on] turned up at our hotel. I didn't see him, but several of the others did. When he saw them, he said: 'Well I never! Are you staying here too?' An agreement had been made between the hotel and the DBU that no Danes would be allowed to stay here at the same time as us, but Borge Tud had registered with a German address. He's as slippery as an eel – and he has the cheek of the devil. But he's not all that sharp, because as soon as the DBU realised he was here they got the hotel to throw him out. I don't know what the idea was of turning up and playing all innocent, but it couldn't have been much fun getting slung out unceremoniously. Our Danish policeman, Erik, gave a nod of recognition and told us that Borge was one of his old customers. As if we didn't know!

I'm turning into a golfing fanatic!

Monday, 15 June

When Simon [a member of the coaching staff] rang to wake me up, I felt as if I'd just fallen asleep. Even though I sleep for eight hours, I'm still completely knocked out in the mornings, and that can make talking to irritating journalists a bit of a problem. They have no idea what to write and their questions get more and more stupid.

Peter Kjaer was asked what it was like to be second reserve goalkeeper, and whether he could accept the idea of being used on the field only now and then, if at all! 'Do you want me to ask Bosse if I can go home?' was Peter's reply. I almost wet myself when I heard him say that!

Some English hooligans have once again done themselves proud by smashing up a town, and because I happen to play in England I get asked for my thoughts on the disturbance. I don't think it's my job to comment on the behaviour of another team's supporters in public, but of course my opinion is that it's a catastrophe. The British police, the government and the FA have done everything they can to prevent trouble at the World Cup, but they must feel like they're banging their heads against a brick wall.

Today I fulfilled one of my big ambitions: I flew in a helicopter. For over half an hour we circled around the area and could see how beautiful the south of France is. This is where I would like to play and live. It's so overwhelmingly beautiful that it almost hurts, and I'm wildly in love with it. And so far I've only scratched the surface!

Tuesday, 16 June

A day off, and for the first time for many years I don't feel in need of one. I feel really fine and full of energy, and I feel like training. I think it has something to do with Jorgen Henriksen's goalkeeper coaching. It's been so long since I last had some proper personal coaching that I've forgotten what good fun and how rewarding it really is.

We had a visit from the press again today. I blew my top at a Dutch TV reporter. He'd come to our hotel to do a story about the Dutch goalkeeper, Edwin van der Sar. He kept on asking me what I thought about van der Sar, and who I thought was the better of the two of us. I told him it didn't really interest me, and that I had difficulty understanding why a Dutch journalist had come to the Danish camp to ask about Dutchmen. Perhaps I seemed arrogant, and maybe it didn't give a very good impression, but I don't think we should be expected to answer all kinds of questions and take part in everything no matter what the angle is.

We had a short team meeting this evening and watched some video of the France–South Africa game. There's no doubt that our game against South Africa will be a difficult one. In the film clips we saw, the South Africans hunted the French all over the pitch, and Jan Borge [a member of the back-up staff] told us that they'd done that for the entire 90 minutes. If we're going to beat them, we'll have to play at our best. I think we will, because the feeling around the camp is really confident, without being arrogant. We think we can do it, but we're aware of the hard work that lies ahead.

Playing cards is still a pleasure.

We're leaving early tomorrow, so now it's time to pack.

Wednesday, 17 June

This has been one of the more uneventful days. Up early this morning, coach to Marseilles, plane to Toulouse, coach to hotel – in brief, one more day of travelling in the life of a footballer.

Another press conference at which *BT*'s Per Steff produced the gem of the day. He told Bosse that several Swedes who know him think he has aged! How amazing! But otherwise the Danish press more or less ask only the obvious questions. Today, as for the past three days, the main subject was the fact that I was about to equal Morten Olsen's record for international appearances. The foreign press are more unpredictable. There were many South African journalists present, and they were very interesting to talk to. They seemed to show respect both for me and the rest of the Danes.

We trained at the stadium at six o'clock that evening, and when we arrived the South Africans hadn't quite finished. I said hello to some of their officials and a couple of players, and they went off saying, 'Good luck, all the best for tomorrow!' in the best sporting tradition. That's always something that warms your heart in the otherwise rather cold world of football.

Thursday, 18 June

A 1–1 draw against South Africa. Not the best result, but we were ahead 1–0 and had several chances to increase our lead.

On the other hand, South Africa wasted one of the best chances anyone has ever wasted against me, so really the result was fair.

I've never in all my life experienced such a bad referee as we had in that game! He dished out three red cards – none of which should have been awarded. But the FIFA referee panel were at the match, and I reckon John Jairo Toro Rendon obviously wanted to impress them. In my opinion, he must surely be thrown on to a plane back to Colombia tomorrow after that performance.

Bente was at the match, and we had a meal together afterwards at the hotel. I was one of the last players to arrive, because once again I was selected for a doping test. I must have been tested about twenty times in all now!

Friday, 19 June

Bente stayed the night here. So did the rest of the girls for that matter, and I think a lot of people had fun in various rooms. We didn't get back until 1.30 this morning, so everyone looked a bit bleary-eyed at breakfast.

Most of us drove our wives or girlfriends around the golf course. Bente agrees with me that we should have some kind of house in the south of France. Whether it should be on a year-round basis or just for holidays we haven't decided yet.

I went for my first swim in the pool, first with Bente, and then later alone. It's really enjoyable when you're feeling a bit flaked out to be able to relax by the pool, read a book or a newspaper, or just do nothing at all. I don't think I'd have any difficulty getting used to a life like that!

It was no surprise that the topic of the day at the press conference was the performance by the referee at yesterday's game. As I was at the doping test after the game, I hadn't had the opportunity to make any comments to the press. But now I have. And I've been told Sepp Blatter has said that the referee had a perfect game.

Saturday, 20 June

Today is my mother's birthday. She is 64, and the old lass is keeping well! At the moment she's in England looking after the children. I've been trying to ring her all day, but no one has been at home. It turned out they'd all been to see a film and then for a meal.

I spent most of the day on the golf course. After training for two hours this morning we got our gear together and did eighteen holes. It took us exactly five hours, after which I went back to the hotel and took a bath in the tub, before I got ready for an evening round of golf. We just managed to finish the second game before it got dark at around half past nine. I had an arrangement to play cards at that time, so the timing was perfect.

The World Cup is progressing, and I'm still enjoying it. Our traumatic experience at the hands of that referee hasn't lessened after having seen the match statistics. We committed exactly six fouls in the whole game and got three yellow and two red cards! The players have asked the DBU to make an official complaint to FIFA, and now we're waiting in suspense to read the DBU's letter.

Sunday, 21 June

No training today. This should not be confused with a day off, because we're going on a sailing trip with all the official guests, together with our wives and girlfriends.

Even though the day is free of training, we can't avoid meeting the press. I felt like staying away, because I didn't feel I had anything to say. But we did our duty, and as the DBU's official letter of complaint was made public just before the press conference, there was a lot to ask about – as far as the press were concerned. I can't say I really agreed, but we're professionals, so I answered politely. But I did manage to get annoyed with a Frenchman who apparently thought he could ask about anything whatsoever and still expect to receive a nice answer.

Anyway, the sailing trip with the girls was good. On our way to the boat we had to visit another square at St Cyr sur Mer where the mayor wanted to greet us again. There were about a thousand people at the square, mostly Danes, and it quickly turned into an autograph session. A lovely start to the day.

We arrived at the boat before the girls, who must have taken a long detour, but finally we were on our way and it turned out to be a very pleasant trip. We sailed around the small bays and also out to sea. It was a beautiful trip which ended when we laid anchor in one of the bays and were served a dreadful lunch. We didn't spend much time over that; most of us were more interested in having a swim. The captain refused to give us permission as he wasn't insured for that kind of thing, but everyone jumped into the water anyway, and it turned out to be great fun. On the way home we sailed past 'Bare-bottom beach', where all the nudists go. No one asked to be dropped off.

We said goodbye to the girls, but as we were still feeling hungry after our lacklustre lunch, we were invited to McDonald's. It must be about two years since I last set foot in one of their restaraunts, and it will be at least another two years before I do so again!

Evening golf was once again on the menu, and I won 800 francs from Jes, Per and Marc. The lads call me the handicap cowboy!

Monday, 22 June

I had big problems sleeping last night, and for that reason my morning call from Simon arrived a couple of hours too early. Why does training last two hours only on days when I'm really tired?

I took a little nap in the afternoon and ended up sleeping for four and a half hours.

I watched the game between England and Romania, which ended 1–2. Dan Petrescu scored the winning goal in extra time, and as he's a member of my dream team I was satisfied. On the other hand, I felt sorry for my English team-mates

David, Paul, Nev and Teddy, who will probably be torn to pieces by the English press tomorrow. But they didn't deserve to win, and they don't look like one of the favourites.

Tuesday, 23 June

It's the day before our game against France, and we are in Lyons. I'm not normally one for whining about travelling by coach, but the trip to Marseilles made me travel-sick and its effects have bothered me all day.

We aren't staying at the best hotel in the world, but it'll do for one night. The food isn't all that good, and we accused Mogens Krogh of being responsible for it, so he's a bit upset. All our teasing is well-meant, but perhaps we go a bit too far now and then.

Bo Johansson is more nervous than I ever thought he could be. He tries to act as if he's calm and has everything under control, but he doesn't convince me. His training session was a little boring, but I don't think he insisted on us playing eleven-a-side all the time to annoy us on purpose. We need a bit of fun to finish off the session, something without too many complications. If we get through to the next round tomorrow, we'll have to have a little chat with him.

After training, Bo called us together for a few words – on the pitch. He didn't think our game during training was satisfactory, and for me that's the first sign of a trainer who's nervous. It must be a long time since he last played himself, because otherwise he would realise that you take it easy at this stage so as not to use up too much energy. But he's right. Our game isn't really together. We're going to play in a new way that we've never really been keen on. We're going to use a 4–3–3 system with the Laudrup brothers up front together with Martin Jorgensen, and that means that we'll be playing without a real striker. Ricardo had also tried that out, without success, because neither Michael nor Brian are finishers. They are more creators and they need someone to make deep runs for them. But we'll have to see how it goes.

Above left Jaap Stam is the rock at the heart of the United defence

Above right In my opinion, Roy Keane is British football's best current midfielder

Right As strong as an ox, Paul Scholes would run through walls for United if necessary

Above left Dwight Yorke is an incredibly buoyant character who has made a huge impact at United

Above right Ryan Giggs is a world-class football star . . . and a thoroughly nice man

Left David Beckham – he has the potential to become one of the greatest United players of all time

Opposite top Bente and the kids watch the Juventus semi-final in Turin

Right Down on the pitch, Dad is celebrating

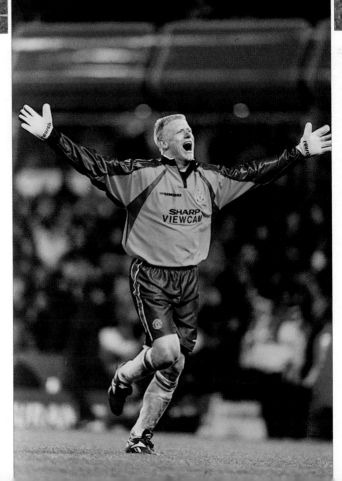

Top left My two children,
Cecilie and Kasper

Bottom left Kasper in
May 1995 – a chip off the
old block

Above and right
Bergkamp's penalty is
saved . . . At the final
whistle, the celebrations
begin

Left The gaffer holds aloft the Premier League trophy, 16 May 1999

Below Proudly holding the FA Cup

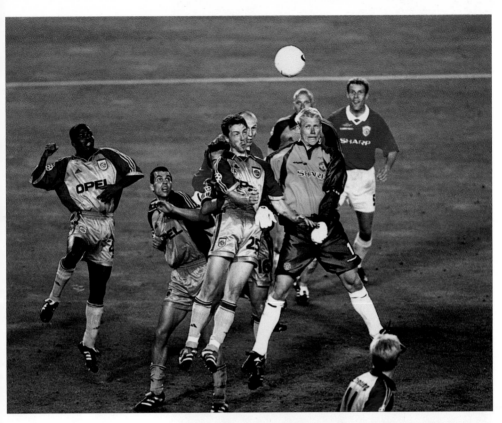

Above It's time for desperate measures!

Right The big one

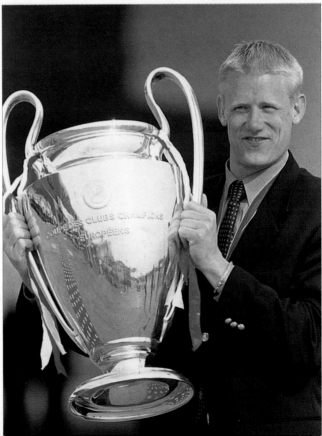

The United fans are special

Wednesday, 24 June

I really shouldn't be writing anything now, because I'm a little bit drunk and I ought to get some sleep. But we didn't get back from Lyons until about midnight, and because of the game it's difficult to go straight to bed without having a lager with the lads.

We lost 2–1 against France. No one can blame us for that, because they're good. In fact, they're really good. But we could have played better. We looked tired, but at least we're through to the next round. Our opponents are going to be Nigeria, who lost against Paraguay today, and I think we have a great chance of getting to the quarter-finals. Today I played my 103rd international. That's a new Danish record, and I really wanted to celebrate the day with a good result.

Our limitations were obvious today. Our right flank just doesn't click, and the sources of information Bosse uses for his match planning have to be questioned, because his tactics proved to be incorrect for the second time running. It's no use making detailed plans to cope with French players who aren't even playing! In my opinion we should play our own game, do the things we're good at, and if they prove to be insufficient, then we'll just have to accept it.

Thursday, 25 June

Simon says he rang to wake me at 8.30 this morning, and that I spoke to him in French, but I don't remember a thing about it. I'd asked him to wake me up because I wanted to get up early to do a spot for TV2, and preferably have it finished by eleven o'clock, because that's when I'd planned to tee off.

Per, Jes and I played nine holes before lunch. At the moment we're really giving each other some hard games, and it's great fun. We grabbed a ten-minute lunch break, then we were back on the course again.

We ate our evening meal at a restaurant in Bandol. Mogens Krogh and Simon had found the place, and they'd been there twice to make perfectly sure the place was all right and that nothing could go wrong. They'd also taken our orders, so the kitchen knew what we were going to eat. But Mogens had dropped a real clanger because he'd translated a dish on the menu as veal, and several of us had ordered it. Unfortunately it turned out to be calf's liver – or calf's balls, as Marc put it so beautifully. This dish proved inedible, and most of it was sent back to the kitchen, which meant that our physiotherapist, Kim, didn't get anything to eat. He complained to Mogens about this several times, but Mogens emphasised that the most important thing was that the players got something to eat. But Kim doesn't like being told he isn't important, so it almost developed into a brawl! Unfortunately the incident was interrupted before we were really given anything to laugh about.

Friday, 26 June

Today is EMMA's birthday. This is our nickname – after the abbreviated form, EM, of the equivalent Danish term for 'European Championship' – for the day six years ago when Denmark became champions of Europe. Normally we throw a big party, but eleven of the players who were in the squad at that time are here in France, and we're in the middle of a tournament. The DBU's management committee sent all EMMA's members a bottle of champagne and a nice letter in order to commemorate the day.

Bosse said we ought to cut down on the training so that it wouldn't take any longer than an hour, but we were kept at it for over an hour and a half, and I have seldom felt so tired. I still think it has something to do with Bosse's nervousness. If a coach is in doubt about anything, he automatically makes you train longer and harder. But the time in between matches is becoming increasingly shorter, so recuperation is a key element.

Jan Borge gave us another lecture at the team meeting and told us all about Nigeria, whom he's seen twice. But when things are shown using the DBU's new editing equipment, it all becomes too theoretical for my liking. In the first place, the quality of the edited film is extremely poor and confusing, and secondly, he shows far too many similar situations. This makes us lose concentration, and the idea behind it all disappears.

I have come right back down to earth again in terms of my golf game and I don't want to talk about it. But our card playing is going great guns.

We leave for Paris tomorrow, so now I'm going to get some sleep.

Saturday, 27 June

It's possible that England haven't impressed anyone in this World Cup, but their song, *Three Lions*, is a certain winner. I think it's world-class.

Brazil and Italy are already through to the quarter-finals after beating Chile and Norway respectively. And we've arrived in Paris to prepare for the match against Nigeria tomorrow. We're staying at a huge hotel called Hotel Concorde la Fayette, which is supposed to be good. It's all right, but it's not the best. But it was here we met Bjarne Riis, the Danish cyclist, after he won the Tour de France, so the place has good Danish traditions.

We've been sightseeing in Paris, but now it's the game against Nigeria that's foremost in our minds. We're really looking forward to it. We've trained on the pitch and it's tip-top, so roll on Sunday!

Sunday, 28 June

It was just one of those normal, routine days today. We won the game 4–1. And it wasn't just the result, but the way in which we achieved it that will be remembered. We played Brazilian football in the best sense of the word, and we have, until further notice, played the best game of the World Cup so far.

We're now sitting on the plane on our way back to Bandol, celebrating in style. That must be enough for today!

Monday, 29 June

The atmosphere at the hotel has been really fantastic today. The result of yesterday's game has echoed around the world, and now everyone's giving us a chance. They've seen that we can play, and it has given our opponents a bit of a shock.

Today it's fun to talk to the press, because it's obvious that our victory, and the fact that it was so convincing, hasn't suited all of them. Now they're actually obliged to show us some respect, and they don't like it. One of them is Jan Jensen of *Ekstra Bladet*, who's been slinging mud at us for months in the worst possible fashion. Today his editorial begins with the words: 'The Danish national team is world-class.' How quickly things change!

Today's newspapers are full of articles about the match, but there's only an absolute minimum of praise for the players. Jes was asked by Ritzau's News Agency if he thought the Nigerians were insultingly inferior, which gives an indication of the kind of attitude the majority of the press has.

Golf beckons, so now I'm going to get some rest so that we can get out on the course early tomorrow morning.

Tuesday, 30 June

England were knocked out by Argentina today, so we've got further in the competition than them. Unfortunately, Beckham was sent off – by the Dane Kim Milton, incidentally – and I thought it was a bit of a shame for my team-mate. But apparently he did something stupid, and he's suffered the consequences. I wouldn't like to be in his shoes tomorrow, because he'll have to take most of the blame for England's exit. But that's the way life is for a superstar!

My great hobby, golf, is posing certain problems. To put it bluntly, I played like a bag of s**t today. I threw away my seven-iron and couldn't find it again, and I knocked the head off my 'Biggest Bertha', which I'd only recently bought for £400. I thought seriously about giving up the game, but I struggled through and ended up hating golf just as much as I have loved it in recent weeks.

But then Per forced me out to play a round of golf in the evening, and I'm pleased he did, because I scored nineteen points in nine holes and I was hitting the ball well again. So perhaps there's a future in it after all?

Wednesday, 1 July

There's not much to report today. I've been feeling very tired and extremely bored.

I've just seen on Teletext that apparently I'm irritable. That must be because I don't often feel like talking to the press. At the moment they want me to say that I'm afraid of all the great Brazilian players. But I'm not, and that means there are no stories for them to write.

Anyway, we'll manage all right!

Thursday, 2 July

We've arrived in Nantes, where the quarter-final is to be played. We're staying at a Novotel, one of a chain of hotels which is apparently a favourite with the organisers. In my mind, it leaves a lot to be desired.

But never mind, we're only going to be here for one night, and then it's back to the Hotel de Fregate and the beautiful golf course.

The press were present in large numbers at the meeting today, and I was asked the most ridiculous question by Torben Larsen from my favourite newspaper, *BT*. He wanted to know, in absolute seriousness, what the most important thing for me would be: to play an entertaining game and lose, or to squeeze a 1–0 victory by not playing such attractive football. Let us remember that the reward we are talking about here is beating Brazil and booking a place in the semi-finals. But Torben Larsen had difficulty understanding that, so I'm looking forward to seeing what he got out of it in the newspaper tomorrow.

For the meantime, *Forza* Denmark!

Friday, 3 July

So now it has happened. Our football adventure is over. We're out of the World Cup after losing 3–2 to the reigning world champions from Brazil. It wasn't because they played us off the pitch – more like the other way round – we just didn't have the small, decisive elements of luck on our side. We played better than they did, and it was our doing that the game turned out to be one of the best games of the World Cup so far.

Earlier today we saw France beat Italy on penalties following a dull goalless affair, which didn't do anything at all for Italy's reputation. At least we can say we lost with honour.

But we should have won. I felt we had far too much respect for them when they attacked, and that cost us two goals. If we had played our normal game, we could have won easily. But names are names after all, and when you're not used to playing against them you find yourself becoming slightly cramped. Ronaldo was a disaster. He lost the ball almost every time he got it, but we still had far too much respect for him. And this gave some of the others more room – Rivaldo, for example, who scored two goals.

At this moment I feel that today we were better than they were. But that's the way life is, and after a few days have gone by and we look back on it I'm certain we'll be proud of what we've achieved. We are good. We have proved it. Now we just need to build on it.

But now I'm going to get a bit more drunk than I already am, and I don't give a damn about this diary any more!

15 Goalkeeping – The Last Line of Defence

'I have a reputation for being loudmouthed and very temperamental. To a certain extent, this is true and I'm comfortable with it. It's not necessarily a bad thing to be temperamental, but you do have to use it in the right way. Early in my career I was receiving a yellow card almost every other game for yelling at the referee or losing control in other ways. I have learnt my lesson. A temper should be used to your own advantage, not to the opponents'. I use mine to stay alert, to stay focused and to feel that I am constantly part of the game, even when I'm not. It works for me and it's essential for me to perform at my best.'

I CLEARLY REMEMBER a particular United game against Liverpool. Stan Collymore was put through on the right just inside the corner of the area. He knew where the goal was, but he didn't know where I was because I came rushing out towards him. Just as he was about to volley, he saw me. He struck the ball perfectly, and I threw myself straight at his shot. The ball hit me right on the thigh and I kept it out of the goal. Naturally it hurt a bit, but I had to get on with the game. I swear I had a bloodshot impression of the ball on my thigh for the next two months, caused by the violent impact.

If I'd received a blow of a similar intensity in the street, for example, I'm certain I would have collapsed. But this was a football game. The adrenalin is rushing around inside your body and your mind is focused 100 per cent on the task of getting a good result, so you only sense pain initially, and then it gets blocked out. But then again that sharp burst of pain is welcome because it tells you your efforts have been successful. For that reason it's a great feeling to throw yourself into a situation and feel the ball, travelling at over 60 mph, hit you in the leg. Your only thought is 'Saved!' That is, after all, what a goalkeeper's there for.

The goalkeeper is the most isolated, and loneliest, player on a team. His game is fundamentally different from that of everyone else. That's why his attitude and the demands made of him are different too. If he makes a mistake, the cost is nearly always high – a goal, or even a match!

It takes a special set of attributes to be a good goalkeeper, both physical and psychological. He needs a certain level of physical robustness in order to make the opposition respect him. Then high levels of speed and agility. Finally, a fantastic ability to concentrate to ensure that he is on his guard for the full duration of the match. This will also help him to bounce straight back after making an error.

Over the years I have learned that it is better to keep things simple and safe than to be spectacular. It can drain the confidence from opponents if you are seen to be keeping things simple and very secure. If a striker sees his goal-bound effort saved with the minimum of fuss, it can be unsettling for them and the goalkeeper has gained the upper hand. This way, I believe goalkeepers are always in better control than when the throw themselves around acrobatically.

After looking closely at my own game, I've concluded that it has actually become gradually less spectacular, not because I've lost my touch as a goalkeeper, but because I don't feel so much need to play to the gallery. I increasingly use my experience and the positional sense that goes with it. This is something that becomes increasingly necessary as the years go by and you lose some of your speed: then you really need to call on that experience to know how to position yourself in all situations.

Of course I also love those completely frantic and unpredictable situations that sometimes crop up in a football match, where you live on your instinct. All rational thought is forgotten, and only one reality exists: that ball must be stopped at all costs. I can give you a very good illustration of what I mean with an example from a game against Everton. A high ball was sent in towards my goal. I was caught slightly off balance and could only push the ball backwards, up into the air. While I was regaining my balance, the ball started to fall. I was unable to move forward to make a catch, but I could see a perfect chance for a soft headed goal was going to present itself to our opponents, and that had to be avoided. I had no choice but to make a move forward as best I could and touch the ball so that it changed direction. Since there was an opponent right in front of me, there was only one thing I could do: parry the ball down on to his feet. It was a completely illogical thing to do, but I had no alternative. I solved one problem by creating another, and the only option I had left after that was to dive towards him before he attempted a volley. I did so, and with my third touch of the ball and within about four or five seconds, I managed to defuse the situation.

In other words, a goalkeeper's most important attributes are physical capability, the ability to concentrate, mental strength, intelligence and, obviously, the desire for perfection. I've never settled for less, and that has been my driving force all the way through my career. A goalkeeper is a highly specialised member of a football team. He probably has the easiest task of analysing the mistakes he makes, and of using them constructively in his constant quest for improvement. Even though no two football matches are identical, there are still many situations and patterns which repeat themselves, and for me mistakes are unacceptable.

When I become aware of a mistake in the course of a match – and there are always one or two, even though they may not always be apparent to the fans or TV viewers and often have no important consequences – I take them home with me in my mind. I think them through, and I work on them during training, until I'm certain about the details and know how to react next time I face the same kind of situation. This is part of the hard and lonely work behind the scenes, but it's work that's essential if you want to be among the best in the world – and I do. I want to stay that way.

I have a reputation for being loudmouthed and very temperamental. To a certain extent, this is true and I'm comfortable with it. It's not necessarily a bad thing to be temperamental, but you do have to use it in the right way. Early in my career I was receiving a yellow card almost every other game for yelling at the referee or losing control in other ways. I have learnt my lesson. A temper should be used to your own advantage, not to the opponents'. I use mine to stay alert, to stay focused and to feel that I am constantly part of the game, even when I'm not. It works for me and it's essential for me to perform at my best.

However, I don't have the definitive solutions. For other

goalkeepers, a strong temper can have the opposite effect. To offer you a complete contrast to myself, in terms of the way we play rather than the quality of our respective games, I cite David Seaman. On a football field, he is probably the most calm, unflappable individual you can imagine. If David was to suddenly start shouting and screaming at his players, and get involved in everything that was going on on the pitch, his world-class performances would, I'm sure, suffer as a result.

I guess we are all different when it comes to finding the right formula for the temperament and personality of a goalkeeper. I was fortunate enough to have found my formula early in my career, and I have followed it ever since. Everywhere I have played it has been accepted and then integrated into the overall playing plan.

I'm absolutely certain that all the great players I found myself playing alongside at Manchester United appreciated that their man at the back was alive and focused. I quickly established a noisy partnership with my two good friends, Steve Bruce and Gary Pallister. I've often been accused of being the most aggressive of the three, and that may very well be the case, but it was really a question of constant three-way communication. Still, Bruce and Pallister often indulged in their own little disputes because neither of them could accept that he'd made a mistake, and on the occasions when sparks really flew there weren't many members of the team who chose to get involved.

I've never regarded the shouting and bickering as a problem. Whether it has been Bruce, Pallister, Neville, Irwin, Olsen, Rieper, Hogh, Henriksen, Johnsen, Colding, Heintze, Berg, May, Nielsen, Stam or Parker (I could go on for ever!), it is always the same way – when the match is over, we are as good friends as we were before we took to the field.

I grant you, I shout a good deal and I'm probably seen to be shouting more than most. But if you take my on-field presence, both visual and verbal, away from me, I would be a quite ordinary goalkeeper. Trust me, I've tried to restrain myself and it just doesn't work.

I'm often accused of being arrogant. In some aspects of football life I am. But it's not a form of arrogance that exists as an integral part of my personality; rather it's produced quite consciously as a part of my match strategy, which is simple: we have to win. You cannot underestimate the power of psychological strength in the midst of a football match. It's of huge importance to me that my opponents are intimidated by my presence between the posts. It doesn't matter whether it's a striker who has broken through alone to face me in a one-on-one situation, or a midfield player lining up a long-range shot. No matter who it is, they have to know that I'm prepared for them 100 per cent, that I'm ready to do anything within my power to prevent them from scoring. I can assure you it's quite possible to undermine an opponent's self-confidence. For that reason I do what I can, but I would never taunt an opponent or intimidate him in any way. That would be unsportsmanlike, not to mention contrary to the ethics which govern the whole idea of playing football at Manchester United. You play the game honestly, with confidence and pride, and that's all.

One of the most important things for a goalkeeper is the ability to shake off mistakes just as soon as they happen. It is inevitable that we all make mistakes, and sometimes you concede a goal as a result. I admit that when I was younger I had great difficulty wiping the slate clean after an error. I was in anguish for the rest of the game. But with my experience and mental strength, a slip or a mistake is unlikely to influence my performance for the rest of the game. If I make a mistake, I quickly re-focus so that the team and I can get on with it. It's a stark fact, after all, that whatever you do you can't turn the clock back and put things right, so it's meaningless to go on thinking about it. So long as you can learn to do this for the duration of the match, you'll be a greater asset to your team; the fact that I can be irritated about it afterwards or later on that evening when I get home is a completely different matter because it doesn't impact on the game.

The many years I spent with Manchester United undoubtedly improved me as a goalkeeper. Before then, when I was playing in Denmark, I was used to the idea that high crosses delivered from the wings were by definition my balls. This was something I thought I could transfer to English conditions without any problems, but that was far from the case, and it didn't take me long to find that out. I found that crosses were of a considerably better quality than I had been used to. In addition to this, I realised that it was quite normal for strikers to make physical challenges in the air, and I wasn't used to that either. I slowly began to accept that I would have to adjust my style of play.

I discovered that it was quite unnecessary for me to run out and jump to catch or clear balls when I had Bruce and Pallister in front of me, both of whom were extremely competent at dealing with these situations. I adjusted my style of play during my first season, and after that the distribution of responsibility worked really well. All the same, I did manage to get out and pluck the ball out of the air every now and then, in order to set up a quick attack, for instance, with a long throw upfield. The element of surprise created by this technique and the way in which it suddenly changes the momentum of the game, resulted in numerous opportunities and several goals during my time at United.

Journalists sometimes ask me what I think my weaknesses are as a goalkeeper. I've always refused to answer questions of this type, and will continue to do so at least until I've stopped playing football. There can never be a reason to give away a list of shortcomings to opponents which they can consult at their leisure. Between you and me, I actually don't think I have any real weaknesses. If I had, I don't think I would have got this far. I believe that my way of playing is the best way; otherwise, I wouldn't play that way. But that doesn't mean that other ways can't be just as effective.

I make every effort to ensure that the opposition isn't presented with any opportunity to score. I do that by directing, yelling, warning, moving players from one position to another. I'm just simply trying to plug any holes before they appear. If the defensive formation is watertight, scoring a goal is very hard indeed.

When I get hold of the ball, I try to create counter-attacking possibilities. It's not always successful, but the tactic unfailingly forces the opponents to turn around and head for their own goal. This can be both strenuous and demoralising, which is all to my advantage. If my early distribution is successful, a goal-scoring opportunity can be created, and that's what football is all about.

I also try to push my team as far up the pitch as possible. Then I can act as a kind of sweeper. The further away from your own goal, the easier it is to defend. But this ploy requires that the goalkeeper is totally alert and has the nerve to play the ball outside his own penalty area. I have always felt comfortable doing this and I think it has been to the advantage of all the teams that I've played for.

I have been lucky enough to win several personal honours, something that I am naturally proud of. Everyone likes to receive recognition for their hard work, but I am still a little sceptical about awards and I try not to attach too much significance to them. It's not because they are not important, it's just that receiving an award is something very personal and no one individual – with the exception, perhaps, of Diego Maradonna in the 1986 World Cup – has ever won anything on his own in this game.

Maybe I'm just rather bashful about the whole award-giving business. I know that when my career finally comes to an end I will gather together all my medals, trophies and awards from the place where they're kept – at the moment they're on display in United's museum – so that I can sit and look at them and reminisce. Even though I enjoy what I am doing now, I am looking forward to that day.

16 Goodbye England

'From the very moment I stepped off the plane, I felt somehow at home. I had a sense of well-being. As the hours went by and I met various representatives from the club, my attitude towards the project grew increasingly positive. They were very nice people, who behaved in a very charming and relaxed way. I discovered I was a really big name in Lisbon, and I was treated with respect. We were taken for a look at the city, and I'm really looking forward to getting to know it.'

'YOU'RE LEAVING US NOW, sir?'
It was the end of the celebrations after we'd won the European Cup. We'd been driven through Manchester in an open-top bus. The ovations we received were overwhelming, and now we were at the MEN Arena in the centre of Manchester. There were 17,000 people in the place, and when the master of ceremonies asked me that question, he was drowned out as people started to whistle like mad. Usually it isn't funny to be whistled at, but I knew this was an expression of loss. They wanted me to stay. In England. At Manchester United. But, yes – I was leaving them now.

Martin Edwards, the chairman of Manchester United, had paid me a visit after that press conference in the autumn of 1998 when I announced I was playing my last season for United. He'd asked me if I was absolutely certain about my decision. I was certain. After completing our magnificent Treble, I was even more sure. Together with my wife and children, I wanted to start a new life. A different life. We're going to have more leisure time now, more time to devote to one another.

But I still want to play football. I feel I have a number of years left – not necessarily at the very highest level, but still at a high level. And certainly under different climatic conditions to those I got used to in England. The idea of another kind of life to Manchester's unpredictable weather, with two matches a week all through the year, became appealing. The Mediterranean sun I experienced during

Denmark's World Cup stay in the south of France, the thought of life in a little village where you can drink a cup of coffee in the square and lazily watch the world go by, became increasingly attractive.

But the season with United had to be completed first. I didn't want my plans for the future to interfere with the team's ambitions and my own ambitions for the season. I wanted to finish my work for United so that there could be no criticism or doubt regarding the extent of my dedication to the club in my final season.

But once it was all over, suddenly ahead of me lay the exploration of all the possibilities open to me, including the final decision about where I was going to play in the future. I was fairly well prepared for this, both from a psychological point of view and also because I had just started working with Soren Lerby, Jesper Olsen, Kevin Moran and Paul Stretford in a firm the four of us own. Paul Stretford is the man who handled my change of clubs, and the story of how this cooperation began is quite interesting.

During my years with Brondby and United I had a Norwegian agent, Rune Hauge. He was involved in the signing of my two contracts with Manchester United, so perhaps he had the feeling he almost owned a part of me. I hadn't informed Rune Hauge beforehand about the press conference I held in November 1998, at which I announced my decision to leave Manchester United, but the news obviously spread very quickly through Europe because while I was on my way home in the car after the press conference the phone rang. It was Rune Hauge, and he was hopping mad. He stormed and raged at me in a way that went far beyond what the extent of his involvement in my affairs entitled him to. In the end I lost my patience, and Rune Hauge slammed down the phone.

Later that evening he phoned again. In between the two calls he'd flown from Zurich to London. He now regretted his behaviour. He'd reconsidered the matter and thought that he'd overreacted. But as far as I was concerned the damage had already been done. His initial reaction had provided me with all the evidence I needed, and I knew I didn't really need him any more. As soon as his way of looking at matters became a question of him feeling he'd been cheated in some way, as opposed to how he could be of assistance to me in future negotiations, our collaboration had to end.

Put simply, in the middle of that hectic season with United, which was the most demanding I had ever experienced, I needed help in looking after my interests, on a practical level and in terms of professional advice, negotiation skills and dealing with contacts and contracts.

Here's a minor example of how this new partnership with Lerby, Olsen, Moran and Stretford worked for me. In the middle of the most hectic period in the spring, I suddenly ran into a problem with British Gas. There was some kind of mix-up concerning payment of my account. One day I received a cheque for £5,000; the next day British Gas informed me that it was me who owed them £5,000. Then a reminder arrived, followed by a notice that they were going to turn off the gas supply. At that stage of the season I simply didn't have the time to sort all this out, so I just handed all the correspondence over to my new partners, and in no time at all the matter was settled. They also took care of a number of other matters which made my life much less worrisome in that busy period.

Perhaps most important of all, they became a trusted inner circle with whom I could talk about my future. We sat down and considered the situation. What did I want to achieve? I made a list of the clubs I would prefer to play for, and investigations began.

Monaco was at the top of my list, followed by Marseilles. These were two areas I'd fallen in love with during the World Cup in 1998. But of course we had to find some alternatives too. We looked into potential opportunities in Italy, and discovered that several Italian clubs were looking to change goalkeeper. I was number two or three on their lists of those they were interested in, which is understandable – I am, after all, 35 years old. Many of these clubs wanted to invest in a goalkeeper they could be certain of keeping for a number of years, not just on a one- or two-year contract. But broadly speaking there was a very encouraging response, and my successful appearances against Inter and Juventus in the Champions' League certainly helped to stir up interest. We had discussions with Udinese, Roma and other Italian clubs, but there were always certain details that didn't really suit me.

There were also some Spanish clubs in the frame, but they ended up more or less making a fool out of me. We were in touch with Mallorca, who were very interested. Their goalkeeper, Carlos Roa, was going to stop playing for them because he was absolutely convinced the world would come to an end in the year 2000. He planned to use the remainder of his precious time in prayer. Apparently, the directors of Mallorca weren't quite as convinced as their goalkeeper that the end of the world was nigh, but they feared there might be a problem if rumours about me possibly joining the club leaked out before they had sorted out terms with Roa.

We were invited to a meeting in Madrid, but were somewhat surprised when we saw their delegation. Real Mallorca's owners also own Malaga, who had just been promoted, but Malaga is a small club without much money. The owners had arrived not with the Mallorca manager, but with the manager of Malaga, and they started to put forward their proposals, but their words fell on deaf ears. After listening for only a few minutes, Paul Stretford stood up and said: 'When are you going to stop taking the piss out of us?' Shortly afterwards we walked out. I totally agreed with Paul. You have to expect a considerably higher level of seriousness from prospective partners.

Sporting Lisbon had also been hovering in the wings since March, but I kept to my decision that I wouldn't talk to anyone until the season was over, for the reasons I've already mentioned. But when the season ended I re-established contact with some people from Sporting, and they proved to have something really interesting to say. I sensed both determination and ambition behind what I heard, and at the same time I developed an impression that they were a group of very pleasant people.

From numerous training camps and holidays I knew what a wonderful country Portugal is. But I decided to go and have a look at things for myself. The conditions for an agreement had been settled. Paul Stretford had once again done his homework and had faxed an agenda for the day's programme in advance to the people in Lisbon.

And the most wonderful thing happened. From the very moment I stepped off the plane, I felt somehow at home. I had a sense of well-being. As the hours went by and I met various representatives from the club, my attitude towards the project grew increasingly positive. They were very nice people, who behaved in a very charming and relaxed way. I discovered I was a really big name in Lisbon, and I was treated with respect. We were taken for a look at the city, and I'm really looking forward to getting to know it. We also visited their stadium, which is big and really impressive. Then, according to Paul Stretford's agenda, it was time to visit a number of places which might be suitable for Bente and I to set up our future home.

Instead, we were driven to the club's headquarters, where their delegation, including the club's legal adviser, was sitting ready to finalise the agreement. Stretford wasn't pleased about this. He insisted that his agenda should be kept to, and they immediately agreed. So we drove out to look at a few potential sites, and it was great. There were a number of places I was sure would suit our lifestyle and meet the requirements of the family.

I wasn't the least bit doubtful when we arrived back at the club's offices. The financial side was spot-on, the conditions were favourable, so I signed the contract and started my career at the club shortly afterwards. As usual, I travelled to Lisbon alone to start training, while Bente and the children waited in Copenhagen.

We've now started training. And the level of ambition I was led to expect is more than apparent. We have a young team with great potential. The majority of players are between 20 and 23 years old, and they're good footballers. But for me it's going to be a completely different task to the one I faced in Manchester.

Sporting Lisbon aren't the Portuguese champions – they finished in fourth position last season – but with a new manager and a number of new signings, including me, the club is aiming to get right back to the top. It's not an unrealistic aim as far as I can see. I'm still a devil for new challenges, and the idea of being the old experienced hand who can bind a new, young team together in a beautiful country on the edge of the Atlantic is a task I'm more than pleased to take on.

It's now August 1999, and I'm thinking back to August 1991 when my situation resembled the one I'm in now. I'm alone in a new country, and my family is once again waiting in Copenhagen for everything to fall into place.

It's always the family that's put in a difficult situation in a footballer's life. Over the years I've made quite a number of demands on Bente, Kasper and Cecilie. In 1991 they had to uproot themselves from Denmark in order to follow me on a journey to Manchester, where I was able to fulfil all my ambitions, winning everything there was to win and finishing at the top as the goalkeeper of Europe's strongest team. In the meantime my family attempted to live a relatively normal life, which can be extremely difficult in this day and age when the attention of the media is so overwhelming in its intensity. I have compared my life to that of a member of a world-famous rock group on a never-ending tour, but for my family it's been different. They had to live a fairly ordinary life, which for them meant adapting themselves to a new culture, learning a new language, establishing new friends and acquaintances, and finding a new social identity.

Now they have to start all over again. After eight years in England, the family is once again uprooting itself and will have to go through a new process of adaptation which will make renewed demands on their patience. Bente is once more faced with the job of mobilising all her energies to organise the move and make a new home for us, while Kasper and Cecilie will have to find new friends and try to settle in a new country. This is no small task, but – and this is what I'm hoping for – there will almost certainly be great benefits for us around the corner.

The whole idea behind this final move is not to change gear

or to reduce speed, but to get the time to relax and to learn how to relax and establish a more enjoyable way of living. That's the point of it all. But there's also a lot of football to be played. My enthusiasm on the pitch and my desire to win is still as strong as when I played for Gladsaxe-Hero, Hvidovre, Brondby, Manchester United and Denmark.

Career Record

Peter Schmeichel's Manchester United appearances in summary

	L	FA	LC	E	CS	T	Cl	GC	GM
91/92	40	3	6	4	—	53	25	40	5
92/93	42	3	2	1	—	48	22	34	2
93/94	40	7	8	4	1	60	24	55	3
94/95	32	7	—	3	1	43	26	25	16
95/96	36	6	1	2	—	45	22	38	4
96/97	36	3	—	9	1	49	21	48	5
97/98	32	4	—	7	1	44	20	34	8
98/99	34	8	—	13	1	56	19	58	7
Total	**292**	**41**	**17**	**43**	**5**	**398**	**179**	**332**	**50**

Key
L = League, FA = FA Cup, LC = League Cup, E = European competition including European Super Cup, CS = Charity Shield, T = Total, Cl = clean sheets, GC = goals conceded, GM = games missed.

Goals: 1
v Rotor Volgograd (UEFA Cup) at Old Trafford, 26 September 1995

Dismissals: 1
v Charlton Athletic (FA Cup) at Old Trafford, 12 March 1994

Substituted: 5
by Gary Walsh v Ipswich Town at Portman Road, 1 May 1994
by Kevin Pilkington v Crystal Palace at Old Trafford, 19 November 1994
by Kevin Pilkington v Tottenham Hotspur at White Hart Lane, 1 January 1996
by Raimond van der Gouw v Newcastle United at Old Trafford, 18 April 1998
by Raimond van der Gouw v Newcastle United at St James' Park, 3 March 1999

Goals conceded per match: 0.834

Clean sheets: 44.97 per cent of total appearances

Most consecutive clean sheets during one season: 5 (4 times)

Season 1991/92

BARCLAYS LEAGUE DIVISION ONE

	P	W	D	L	F	A	Pts
Leeds United	42	22	16	4	74	37	87
Manchester United	**42**	**21**	**15**	**6**	**63**	**33**	**78**
Sheffield Wednesday	42	21	12	9	62	49	75
Arsenal	42	19	15	8	81	46	72
Manchester City	42	20	10	12	61	48	70
Liverpool	42	16	16	10	47	40	64
Aston Villa	42	17	9	16	48	44	60
Nottingham Forest	42	16	11	15	60	58	59
Sheffield United	42	16	9	17	65	63	57
Crystal Palace	42	14	15	13	53	61	57
QPR	42	12	18	12	48	47	54
Everton	42	13	14	15	52	51	53
Wimbledon	42	13	14	15	53	53	53
Chelsea	42	13	14	15	50	60	53
Tottenham Hotspur	42	15	7	20	58	63	52
Southampton	42	14	10	18	39	55	52
Oldham Athletic	42	14	9	19	63	67	51
Norwich City	42	11	12	19	47	63	45
Coventry City	42	11	11	20	35	44	44
Luton Town	42	10	12	20	38	71	42
Notts County	42	10	10	22	40	62	40
West Ham United	42	9	11	22	37	59	38

Schmeichel's appearances

(in League except where noted)

Date	Opponents	Venue	Score	
Aug 17	Notts County	Old Trafford	Won 2–0	
Aug 21	Aston Villa	Villa Park	Won 1–0	
Aug 24	Everton	Goodison Park	Drew 0–0	
Aug 28	Oldham Athletic	Old Trafford	Won 1–0	
Aug 31	Leeds United	Old Trafford	Drew 1–1	
Sept 3	Wimbledon	Selhurst Park	Won 2–1	
Sept 7	Norwich City	Old Trafford	Won 3–0	
Sept 14	Southampton	The Dell	Won 1–0	
Sept 18	PAE Athinaikos	Athens	Drew 0–0	ECWC
Sept 21	Luton Town	Old Trafford	Won 5–0	
Sept 28	Tottenham Hotspur	White Hart Lane	Won 2–1	
Oct 2	PAE Athinaikos	Old Trafford	Won 2–0	ECWC
Oct 6	Liverpool	Old Trafford	Drew 0–0	
Oct 19	Arsenal	Old Trafford	Drew 1–1	
Oct 23	Atletico Madrid	Madrid	Lost 0–3	ECWC
Oct 26	Sheffield Wed.	Hillsborough	Lost 2–3	
Oct 30	Portsmouth	Old Trafford	Won 3–1	RLC
Nov 2	Sheffield United	Old Trafford	Won 2–0	

Nov 16	Manchester City	Maine Road	Drew 0–0	
Nov 19	Red Star Belgrade	Old Trafford	Won 1–0	ESC
Nov 23	West Ham United	Old Trafford	Won 2–1	
Nov 30	Crystal Palace	Selhurst Park	Won 3–1	
Dec 4	Oldham Athletic	Old Trafford	Won 2–0	RLC
Dec 7	Coventry City	Old Trafford	Won 4–0	
Dec 15	Chelsea	Stamford Bridge	Won 3–1	
Dec 26	Oldham Athletic	Boundary Park	Won 6–3	
Dec 29	Leeds United	Elland Road	Drew 1–1	
Jan 1	QPR	Old Trafford	Lost 1–4	
Jan 8	Leeds United	Elland Road	Won 3–1	RLC
Jan 11	Everton	Old Trafford	Won 1–0	
Jan 15	Leeds United	Elland Road	Won 1–0	FA
Jan 18	Notts County	Meadow Lane	Drew 1–1	
Jan 22	Aston Villa	Old Trafford	Won 1–0	
Jan 27	Southampton	The Dell	Drew 0–0	FA
Feb 1	Arsenal	Highbury	Drew 1–1	
Feb 5	Southampton	Old Trafford	Drew 2–2	FA
			Lost 2–4 on pens	
Feb 8	Sheffield Wed.	Old Trafford	Drew 1–1	
Feb 22	Crystal Palace	Old Trafford	Won 2–0	
Mar 4	Middlesbrough	Ayresome Park	Drew 0–0	RLC
Mar 11	Middlesbrough	Old Trafford	Won 2–1	RLC
Mar 14	Sheffield United	Bramall Lane	Won 2–1	
Mar 18	Notts Forest	City Ground	Lost 0–1	
Mar 21	Wimbledon	Old Trafford	Drew 0–0	
Mar 28	QPR	Loftus Road	Drew 0–0	
Mar 31	Norwich City	Carrow Road	Won 3–1	
April 7	Manchester City	Old Trafford	Drew 1–1	
April 12	Notts Forest	Wembley	Won 1–0	RLCF
April 16	Southampton	Old Trafford	Won 1–0	
April 18	Luton Town	Kenilworth Road	Drew 1–1	
April 20	Notts Forest	Old Trafford	Lost 1–2	
April 22	West Ham United	Upton Park	Lost 0–1	
April 26	Liverpool	Anfield	Lost 0–2	
May 2	Tottenham Hotspur	Old Trafford	Won 3–1	

Key
ECWC = European Cup-Winners' Cup, RLC = Rumbelows League Cup,
ESC = European Super Cup, FA = FA Cup, RLCF = Rumbelows League Cup
final

Season 1992/93

FA PREMIER LEAGUE

	P	W	D	L	F	A	Pts
Manchester United	**42**	**24**	**12**	**6**	**67**	**31**	**84**
Aston Villa	42	21	11	10	57	40	74
Norwich City	42	21	9	12	61	65	72
Blackburn Rovers	42	20	11	11	68	46	71
QPR	42	17	12	13	63	55	63
Liverpool	42	16	11	15	62	55	59
Sheffield Wednesday	42	15	14	13	55	51	59
Tottenham Hotspur	42	16	11	15	60	66	59
Manchester City	42	15	12	15	56	51	57
Arsenal	42	15	11	16	40	38	56
Chelsea	42	14	14	14	51	54	56
Wimbledon	42	14	12	16	56	55	54
Everton	42	15	8	19	53	55	53
Sheffield United	42	14	10	18	54	53	52
Coventry City	42	13	13	16	52	57	52
Ipswich Town	42	12	16	14	50	55	52
Leeds United	42	12	15	15	57	62	51
Southampton	42	13	11	18	54	61	50
Oldham Athletic	42	13	10	19	63	74	49
Crystal Palace	42	11	16	15	48	61	49
Middlesbrough	42	11	11	20	54	75	44
Nottingham Forest	42	10	10	22	41	62	40

Schmeichel's appearances

(in League except where noted)

Date	Opponents	Venue	Score	
Aug 15	Sheffield United	Bramall Lane	Lost 1–2	
Aug 19	Everton	Old Trafford	Lost 0–3	
Aug 22	Ipswich Town	Old Trafford	Drew 1–1	
Aug 24	Southampton	The Dell	Won 1–0	
Aug 29	Notts Forest	City Ground	Won 2–0	
Sept 2	Crystal Palace	Old Trafford	Won 1–0	
Sept 6	Leeds United	Old Trafford	Won 2–0	
Sept 12	Everton	Goodison Park	Won 2–0	
Sept 19	Tottenham Hotspur	White Hart Lane	Drew 1–1	
Sept 26	QPR	Old Trafford	Drew 0–0	
Sept 29	Torpedo Moscow	Moscow	Drew 0–0	UEFA
			Lost 3–4 on pens	
Oct 3	Middlesbrough	Ayresome Park	Drew 1–1	
Oct 7	Brighton	Old Trafford	Won 1–0	CCLC
Oct 18	Liverpool	Old Trafford	Drew 2–2	
Oct 24	Blackburn Rovers	Ewood Park	Drew 0–0	
Oct 28	Aston Villa	Villa Park	Lost 0–1	CCLC
Oct 31	Wimbledon	Old Trafford	Lost 0–1	

Nov 7	Aston Villa	Villa Park	Lost 0–1	
Nov 21	Oldham Athletic	Old Trafford	Won 3–0	
Nov 28	Arsenal	Highbury	Won 1–0	
Dec 6	Manchester City	Old Trafford	Won 2–1	
Dec 12	Norwich City	Old Trafford	Won 1–0	
Dec 19	Chelsea	Stamford Bridge	Drew 1–1	
Dec 26	Sheffield Wed.	Hillsborough	Drew 3–3	
Dec 28	Coventry City	Old Trafford	Won 5–0	
Jan 5	Bury	Old Trafford	Won 2–0	FA
Jan 9	Tottenham Hotspur	Old Trafford	Won 4–1	
Jan 18	QPR	Loftus Road	Won 3–1	
Jan 23	Brighton	Old Trafford	Won 1–0	FA
Jan 27	Notts Forest	Old Trafford	Won 2–0	
Jan 30	Ipswich Town	Portman Road	Lost 1–2	
Feb 6	Sheffield United	Old Trafford	Won 2–1	
Feb 8	Leeds United	Elland Road	Drew 0–0	
Feb 14	Sheffield United	Bramall Lane	Lost 1–2	FA
Feb 20	Southampton	Old Trafford	Won 2–1	
Feb 27	Middlesbrough	Old Trafford	Won 3–0	
Mar 6	Liverpool	Anfield	Won 2–1	
Mar 9	Oldham Athletic	Boundary Park	Lost 0–1	
Mar 14	Aston Villa	Old Trafford	Drew 1–1	
Mar 20	Manchester City	Maine Road	Drew 1–1	
Mar 24	Arsenal	Old Trafford	Drew 0–0	
April 5	Norwich City	Carrow Road	Won 3–1	
April 10	Sheffield Wed.	Old Trafford	Won 2–1	
April 12	Coventry City	Highfield Road	Won 1–0	
April 17	Chelsea	Old Trafford	Won 3–0	
April 21	Crystal Palace	Selhurst Park	Won 2–0	
May 3	Blackburn Rovers	Old Trafford	Won 3–1	
May 9	Wimbledon	Selhurst Park	Won 2–1	

Key
UEFA = UEFA Cup, CCLC = Coca-Cola League Cup, FA = FA Cup

Season 1993/94

FA CARLING PREMIERSHIP

	P	W	D	L	F	A	Pts
Manchester United	**42**	**27**	**11**	**4**	**80**	**38**	**92**
Blackburn Rovers	42	25	9	8	63	36	84
Newcastle United	42	23	8	11	82	41	77
Arsenal	42	18	17	7	53	28	71
Leeds United	42	18	16	8	65	39	70
Wimbledon	42	18	11	13	56	53	65
Sheffield Wednesday	42	16	16	10	76	54	64
Liverpool	42	17	9	16	59	55	60
QPR	42	16	12	14	62	61	60
Aston Villa	42	15	12	15	46	50	57
Coventry City	42	14	14	14	43	45	56
Norwich City	42	12	17	13	65	61	53
West Ham United	42	13	13	16	47	58	52
Chelsea	42	13	12	17	49	53	51
Tottenham Hotspur	42	11	12	19	54	59	45
Manchester City	42	9	18	15	38	49	45
Everton	42	12	8	22	42	63	44
Southampton	42	12	7	23	49	66	43
Ipswich Town	42	9	16	17	35	58	43
Sheffield United	42	8	18	16	42	60	42
Oldham Athletic	42	10	13	19	42	68	40
Swindon Town	42	5	15	22	47	100	30

Schmeichel's appearances

(in League except where noted)

Date	Opponents	Venue	Score	
Aug 7	Arsenal	Wembley	Drew 1–1	CS
			won 5–4 on pens	
Aug 15	Norwich City	Carrow Road	Won 2–0	
Aug 18	Sheffield United	Old Trafford	Won 3–0	
Aug 21	Newcastle United	Old Trafford	Drew 1–1	
Aug 23	Aston Villa	Villa Park	Won 2–1	
Aug 28	Southampton	The Dell	Won 3–1	
Sept 1	West Ham United	Old Trafford	Won 3–0	
Sept 11	Chelsea	Stamford Bridge	Lost 0–1	
Sept 15	Kispest-Honved	Budapest	Won 3–2	EC
Sept 19	Arsenal	Old Trafford	Won 1–0	
Sept 22	Stoke City	Victoria Ground	Lost 1–2	CCLC
Sept 25	Swindon Town	Old Trafford	Won 4–2	
Sept 29	Kispest-Honved	Old Trafford	Won 2–1	EC
Oct 2	Sheffield Wed.	Hillsborough	Won 3–2	
Oct 6	Stoke City	Old Trafford	Won 2–0	CCLC
Oct 16	Tottenham Hotspur	Old Trafford	Won 2–1	
Oct 20	Galatasaray	Old Trafford	Drew 3–3	EC

Oct 23	Everton	Goodison Park	Won 1–0	
Oct 27	Leicester City	Old Trafford	Won 5–1	CCLC
Oct 30	QPR	Old Trafford	Won 2–1	
Nov 3	Galatasaray	Istanbul	Drew 0–0 lost on away goals	EC
Nov 7	Manchester City	Maine Road	Won 3–2	
Nov 20	Wimbledon	Old Trafford	Won 3–1	
Nov 24	Ipswich Town	Old Trafford	Drew 0–0	
Nov 27	Coventry City	Highfield Road	Won 1–0	
Nov 30	Everton	Goodison Park	Won 2–0	CCLC
Dec 4	Norwich City	Old Trafford	Drew 2–2	
Dec 7	Sheffield United	Bramall Lane	Won 3–0	
Dec 11	Newcastle United	St James' Park	Drew 1–1	
Dec 19	Aston Villa	Old Trafford	Won 3–1	
Dec 26	Blackburn Rovers	Old Trafford	Drew 1–1	
Dec 29	Oldham Athletic	Boundary Park	Won 5–2	
Jan 1	Leeds United	Old Trafford	Drew 0–0	
Jan 4	Liverpool	Anfield	Drew 3–3	
Jan 9	Sheffield United	Bramall Lane	Won 1–0	FA
Jan 12	Portsmouth	Old Trafford	Drew 2–2	CCLC
Jan 15	Tottenham Hotspur	White Hart Lane	Won 1–0	
Jan 22	Everton	Old Trafford	Won 1–0	
Jan 26	Portsmouth	Fratton Park	Won 1–0	CCLC
Jan 30	Norwich City	Carrow Road	Won 2–0	FA
Feb 5	QPR	Loftus Road	Won 3–2	
Feb 13	Sheffield Wed.	Old Trafford	Won 1–0	CCLC
Feb 20	Wimbledon	Selhurst Park	Won 3–0	FA
Feb 26	West Ham United	Upton Park	Drew 2–2	
March 2	Sheffield Wed.	Hillsborough	Won 4–2	CCLC
March 5	Chelsea	Old Trafford	Lost 0–1	
March 12	Charlton Athletic	Old Trafford	Won 3–1	FA
March 16	Sheffield Wed.	Old Trafford	Won 5–0	
March 19	Swindon Town	County Ground	Drew 2–2	
March 22	Arsenal	Highbury	Drew 2–2	
March 30	Liverpool	Old Trafford	Won 1–0	
April 2	Blackburn Rovers	Ewood Park	Lost 0–2	
April 4	Oldham Athletic	Old Trafford	Won 3–2	
April 10	Oldham Athletic	Wembley	Drew 1–1	FA
April 13	Oldham Athletic	Maine Road	Won 4–1	FA
April 16	Wimbledon	Selhurst Park	Lost 0–1	
April 23	Manchester City	Old Trafford	Won 2–0	
April 27	Leeds United	Elland Road	Won 2–0	
May 1	Ipswich Town	Portman Road	Won 2–1	
May 14	Chelsea	Wembley	Won 4–0	FAF

Key
CS = Charity Shield, EC = European Cup, CCLC = Coca-Cola League Cup,
FAF = FA Cup final

Season 1994/95

FA CARLING PREMIERSHIP

	P	W	D	L	F	A	Pts
Blackburn Rovers	42	27	8	7	80	39	89
Manchester United	**42**	**26**	**10**	**6**	**77**	**28**	**88**
Nottingham Forest	42	22	11	9	72	43	77
Liverpool	42	21	11	10	65	37	74
Leeds United	42	20	13	9	59	38	73
Newcastle United	42	20	12	10	67	47	72
Tottenham Hotspur	42	16	14	12	66	58	62
QPR	42	17	9	16	61	59	60
Wimbledon	42	15	11	16	48	65	56
Southampton	42	12	18	12	61	63	54
Chelsea	42	13	15	14	50	55	54
Arsenal	42	13	12	17	52	49	51
Sheffield Wednesday	42	13	12	17	49	57	51
West Ham United	42	13	11	18	44	48	50
Everton	42	11	17	14	44	51	50
Coventry City	42	12	14	16	44	62	50
Manchester City	42	12	13	17	53	64	49
Aston Villa	42	11	15	16	51	56	48
Crystal Palace	42	11	12	19	34	49	45
Norwich City	42	10	13	19	37	54	43
Leicester City	42	6	11	25	45	80	29
Ipswich Town	42	7	6	29	36	93	27

EUROPEAN CHAMPIONS' LEAGUE GROUP A

	P	W	D	L	F	A	Pts
IFK Gothenburg	6	4	1	1	10	7	9
Barcelona	6	2	2	2	11	8	6
Manchester United	**6**	**2**	**2**	**2**	**11**	**11**	**6**
Galatasaray	6	1	1	4	3	9	3

Schmeichel's appearances

(in League except where noted)

Date	Opponents	Venue	Score	
Aug 14	Blackburn Rovers	Wembley	Won 2–0	CS
Aug 20	QPR	Old Trafford	Won 2–0	
Aug 22	Notts Forest	City Ground	Drew 1–1	
Aug 27	Tottenham Hotspur	White Hart Lane	Won 1–0	
Aug 31	Wimbledon	Old Trafford	Won 3–0	
Sept 11	Leeds United	Elland Road	Lost 1–2	
Sept 14	IFK Gothenburg	Old Trafford	Won 4–2	ECL
Sept 17	Liverpool	Old Trafford	Won 2–0	
Sept 28	Galatasaray	Istanbul	Drew 0–0	ECL
Oct 1	Everton	Old Trafford	Won 2–0	

Oct 8	Sheffield Wed.	Hillsborough	Lost 0–1	
Oct 15	West Ham United	Old Trafford	Won 1–0	
Oct 19	Barcelona	Old Trafford	Drew 2–2	ECL
Oct 23	Blackburn Rovers	Ewood Park	Won 4–2	
Oct 29	Newcastle United	Old Trafford	Won 2–0	
Nov 10	Manchester City	Old Trafford	Won 5–0	
Nov 19	Crystal Palace	Old Trafford	Won 3–0	
Jan 9	Sheffield United	Bramall Lane	Won 2–0	FA
Jan 15	Newcastle United	St James' Park	Drew 1–1	
Jan 22	Blackburn Rovers	Old Trafford	Won 1–0	
Jan 25	Crystal Palace	Selhurst Park	Drew 1–1	
Jan 28	Wrexham	Old Trafford	Won 5–2	FA
Feb 4	Aston Villa	Old Trafford	Won 1–0	
Feb 11	Manchester City	Maine Road	Won 3–0	
Feb 19	Leeds United	Old Trafford	Won 3–1	FA
Feb 22	Norwich City	Carrow Road	Won 2–0	
Feb 25	Everton	Goodison Park	Lost 0–1	
Mar 4	Ipswich Town	Old Trafford	Won 9–0	
Mar 7	Wimbledon	Selhurst Park	Won 1–0	
Mar 12	QPR	Old Trafford	Won 2–0	FA
Mar 15	Tottenham Hotspur	Old Trafford	Drew 0–0	
Mar 19	Liverpool	Anfield	Lost 0–2	
Mar 22	Arsenal	Old Trafford	Won 3–0	
April 2	Leeds United	Old Trafford	Drew 0–0	
April 9	Crystal Palace	Villa Park	Drew 2–2	FA
April 12	Crystal Palace	Villa Park	Won 2–0	FA
April 15	Leicester City	Filbert Street	Won 4–0	
April 17	Chelsea	Old Trafford	Drew 0–0	
May 1	Coventry City	Highfield Road	Won 3–2	
May 7	Sheffield Wed.	Old Trafford	Won 1–0	
May 10	Southampton	Old Trafford	Won 2–1	
May 14	West Ham United	Upton Park	Drew 1–1	
May 20	Everton	Wembley	Lost 0–1	FAF

Key

CS = Charity Shield, ECL = European Champions' League, FA = FA Cup,
FAF = FA Cup final

Season 1995/96

FA CARLING PREMIERSHIP

	P	W	D	L	F	A	Pts
Manchester United	**38**	**25**	**7**	**6**	**73**	**35**	**82**
Newcastle United	38	24	6	8	66	37	78
Liverpool	38	20	11	7	70	34	71
Aston Villa	38	18	9	11	52	35	63
Arsenal	38	17	12	9	49	32	63
Everton	38	17	10	11	64	44	61
Blackburn Rovers	38	18	7	13	61	47	61
Tottenham Hotspur	38	16	13	9	50	38	61
Nottingham Forest	38	15	13	10	50	54	58
West Ham United	38	14	9	15	43	52	51
Chelsea	38	12	14	12	46	44	50
Middlesbrough	38	11	10	17	35	50	43
Leeds United	38	12	7	19	40	57	43
Wimbledon	38	10	11	17	55	70	41
Sheffield Wednesday	38	10	10	18	48	61	40
Coventry City	38	8	14	16	42	60	38
Southampton	38	9	11	18	34	52	38
Manchester City	38	9	11	18	33	58	38
QPR	38	9	6	23	38	57	33
Bolton Wanderers	38	8	5	25	39	71	29

Schmeichel's appearances

(in League except where noted)

Date	Opponents	Venue	Score	
Aug 19	Aston Villa	Villa Park	Lost 1–3	
Aug 23	West Ham United	Old Trafford	Won 2–1	
Aug 26	Wimbledon	Old Trafford	Won 3–1	
Aug 28	Blackburn Rovers	Ewood Park	Won 2–1	
Sept 9	Everton	Goodison Park	Won 3–2	
Sept 12	Rotor Volgograd	Volgograd	Drew 0–0	UEFA
Sept 16	Bolton Wanderers	Old Trafford	Won 3–0	
Sept 23	Sheffield Wed.	Hillsborough	Drew 0–0	
Sept 26	Rotor Volgograd	Old Trafford	Drew 2–2	UEFA
			lost on away goals	
Oct 1	Liverpool	Old Trafford	Drew 2–2	
Oct 3	York City	Bootham Crescent	Won 3–1	CCLC
Oct 14	Manchester City	Old Trafford	Won 1–0	
Oct 21	Chelsea	Stamford Bridge	Won 4–1	
Oct 28	Middlesbrough	Old Trafford	Won 2–0	
Nov 4	Arsenal	Highbury	Lost 0–1	
Nov 18	Southampton	Old Trafford	Won 4–1	
Nov 22	Coventry City	Highfield Road	Won 4–0	
Nov 27	Notts Forest	City Ground	Drew 1–1	
Dec 17	Liverpool	Anfield	Lost 0–2	

Dec 24	Leeds United	Elland Road	Lost 1–3	
Dec 27	Newcastle United	Old Trafford	Won 2–0	
Dec 30	QPR	Old Trafford	Won 2–1	
Jan 1	Tottenham Hotspur	White Hart Lane	Lost 1–4	
Jan 13	Aston Villa	Old Trafford	Drew 0–0	
Jan 16	Sunderland	Roker Park	Won 2–1	FA
Jan 22	West Ham United	Upton Park	Won 1–0	
Jan 27	Reading	Elm Park	Won 3–0	FA
Feb 3	Wimbledon	Selhurst Park	Won 4–2	
Feb 10	Blackburn Rovers	Old Trafford	Won 1–0	
Feb 18	Manchester City	Old Trafford	Won 2–1	FA
Feb 21	Everton	Old Trafford	Won 2–0	
Feb 25	Bolton Wanderers	Burnden Park	Won 6–0	
Mar 4	Newcastle United	St James' Park	Won 1–0	
Mar 11	Southampton	Old Trafford	Won 2–0	FA
Mar 16	QPR	Loftus Road	Drew 1–1	
Mar 20	Arsenal	Old Trafford	Won 1–0	
Mar 24	Tottenham Hotspur	Old Trafford	Won 1–0	
Mar 31	Chelsea	Villa Park	Won 2–1	FA
April 6	Manchester City	Maine Road	Won 3–2	
April 8	Coventry City	Old Trafford	Won 1–0	
April 13	Southampton	The Dell	Lost 1–3	
April 17	Leeds United	Old Trafford	Won 1–0	
April 28	Notts Forest	Old Trafford	Won 5–0	
May 5	Middlesbrough	The Riverside	Won 3–0	
May 11	Liverpool	Wembley	Won 1–0	FAF

Key
UEFA = UEFA Cup, CCLC = Coca-Cola League Cup, FA = FA Cup, FAF = FA
Cup final

Season 1996/97
FA Carling Premiership

	P	W	D	L	F	A	Pts
Manchester United	**38**	**21**	**12**	**5**	**76**	**44**	**75**
Newcastle United	38	19	11	8	73	40	68
Arsenal	38	19	11	8	62	32	68
Liverpool	38	19	11	8	62	37	68
Aston Villa	38	17	10	11	47	34	61
Chelsea	38	16	11	11	58	55	59
Sheffield Wednesday	38	14	15	9	50	51	57
Wimbledon	38	15	11	12	49	46	56
Leicester City	38	12	11	15	46	54	47
Tottenham Hotspur	38	13	7	18	44	51	46
Leeds United	38	11	13	14	28	38	46
Derby County	38	11	13	14	45	58	46
Blackburn Rovers	38	9	15	14	42	43	42
West Ham United	38	10	12	16	39	48	42
Everton	38	10	12	16	44	57	42
Southampton	38	10	11	17	50	56	41
Coventry City	38	9	14	15	38	54	41
Sunderland	38	10	10	18	35	53	40
Middlesbrough*	38	10	12	16	51	60	39
Nottingham Forest	38	6	16	16	31	59	34

*3 points deducted for failing to fulfil a fixture

European Champions' League Group C

	P	W	D	L	F	A	Pts
Juventus	6	5	1	0	11	1	16
Manchester United	**6**	**3**	**0**	**3**	**6**	**3**	**9**
Fenerbahce	6	2	1	3	3	6	7
Rapid Vienna	6	0	2	4	2	12	2

Quarter-final: Manchester United beat FC Porto 4–0 on aggregate
Semi-final: Manchester United lost to Borussia Dortmund 0–2 on aggregate

Schmeichel's appearances
(in League except where noted)

Date	Opponents	Venue	Score	
Aug 11	Newcastle United	Wembley	Won 4–0	CS
Aug 17	Wimbledon	Selhurst Park	Won 3–0	
Aug 21	Everton	Old Trafford	Drew 2–2	
Aug 25	Blackburn Rovers	Old Trafford	Drew 2–2	
Sept 4	Derby County	Baseball Ground	Drew 1–1	
Sept 7	Leeds United	Elland Road	Won 4–0	
Sept 11	Juventus	Turin	Lost 0–1	ECL
Sept 14	Notts Forest	Old Trafford	Won 4–1	

Sept 25	Rapid Vienna	Old Trafford	Won 2–0	ECL
Sept 29	Tottenham Hotspur	Old Trafford	Won 2–0	
Oct 12	Liverpool	Old Trafford	Won 1–0	
Oct 16	Fenerbahce	Istanbul	Won 2–0	ECL
Oct 20	Newcastle United	St James' Park	Lost 0–5	
Oct 26	Southampton	The Dell	Lost 3–6	
Oct 30	Fenerbahce	Old Trafford	Lost 0–1	ECL
Nov 2	Chelsea	Old Trafford	Lost 1–2	
Nov 16	Arsenal	Old Trafford	Won 1–0	
Nov 20	Juventus	Old Trafford	Lost 0–1	ECL
Nov 23	Middlesbrough	The Riverside	Drew 2–2	
Nov 30	Leicester City	Old Trafford	Won 3–1	
Dec 4	Rapid Vienna	Vienna	Won 2–0	ECL
Dec 8	West Ham United	Upton Park	Drew 2–2	
Dec 18	Sheffield Wed.	Hillsborough	Drew 1–1	
Dec 21	Sunderland	Old Trafford	Won 5–0	
Dec 26	Notts Forest	City Ground	Won 4–0	
Dec 28	Leeds United	Old Trafford	Won 1–0	
Jan 1	Aston Villa	Old Trafford	Drew 0–0	
Jan 5	Tottenham Hotspur	Old Trafford	Won 2–0	FA
Jan 12	Tottenham Hotspur	White Hart Lane	Won 2–1	
Jan 18	Coventry City	Highfield Road	Won 2–0	
Jan 25	Wimbledon	Old Trafford	Drew 1–1	FA
Jan 29	Wimbledon	Old Trafford	Won 2–1	
Feb 1	Southampton	Old Trafford	Won 2–1	
Feb 4	Wimbledon	Selhurst Park	Lost 0–1	FA
Feb 19	Arsenal	Highbury	Won 2–1	
Feb 22	Chelsea	Stamford Bridge	Drew 1–1	
Mar 1	Coventry City	Old Trafford	Won 3–1	
Mar 5	FC Porto	Old Trafford	Won 4–0	ECL
Mar 8	Sunderland	Roker Park	Lost 1–2	
Mar 15	Sheffield Wed.	Old Trafford	Won 2–0	
Mar 19	FC Porto	Porto	Drew 0–0	ECL
Mar 22	Everton	Goodison Park	Won 2–0	
April 5	Derby County	Old Trafford	Lost 2–3	
April 23	Borussia Dortmund	Old Trafford	Lost 0–1	ECL
April 19	Liverpool	Anfield	Won 3–1	
May 3	Leicester City	Filbert Street	Drew 2–2	
May 5	Middlesbrough	Old Trafford	Drew 3–3	
May 8	Newcastle United	Old Trafford	Drew 0–0	
May 11	West Ham United	Old Trafford	Won 2–0	

Key
CS = Charity Shield, ECL = European Champions' League, FA = FA Cup

Season 1997/98
FA CARLING PREMIERSHIP

	P	W	D	L	F	A	Pts
Arsenal	38	23	9	6	68	33	78
Manchester United	**38**	**23**	**8**	**7**	**73**	**26**	**77**
Liverpool	38	18	11	9	68	42	65
Chelsea	38	20	3	15	71	43	63
Leeds United	38	17	8	13	57	46	59
Blackburn Rovers	38	16	10	12	57	52	58
Aston Villa	38	17	6	15	49	48	57
West Ham United	38	16	8	14	56	57	56
Derby County	38	16	7	15	52	49	55
Leicester City	38	13	14	11	51	41	53
Coventry City	38	12	16	10	46	44	52
Southampton	38	14	6	18	50	55	48
Newcastle United	38	11	11	16	35	44	44
Tottenham Hotspur	38	11	11	16	44	56	44
Wimbledon	38	10	14	14	34	46	44
Sheffield Wednesday	38	12	8	18	52	67	44
Everton	38	9	13	16	41	56	40
Bolton Wanderers	38	9	13	16	41	61	40
Barnsley	38	10	5	23	37	82	35
Crystal Palace	38	8	9	21	37	71	33

EUROPEAN CHAMPIONS' LEAGUE GROUP B

	P	W	D	L	F	A	Pts
Manchester United	**6**	**5**	**0**	**1**	**14**	**5**	**15**
Juventus	6	4	0	2	12	8	12
Feyenoord	6	3	0	3	8	10	9
FC Kosice	6	0	0	6	2	13	0

Quarter-final: Manchester United drew with AS Monaco 1–1 on aggregate, lost on away goals

Schmeichel's appearances
(in League except where noted)

Date	Opponents	Venue	Score	
Aug 3	Chelsea	Wembley	Drew 1–1 won 4–2 on pens	CS
Aug 10	Tottenham Hotspur	White Hart Lane	Won 2–0	
Aug 13	Southampton	Old Trafford	Won 1–0	
Aug 23	Leicester City	Filbert Street	Drew 0–0	
Aug 27	Everton	Goodison Park	Won 2–0	
Aug 30	Coventry City	Old Trafford	Won 3–0	
Sept 13	West Ham United	Old Trafford	Won 2–1	
Sept 17	FC Kosice	Kosice	Won 3–0	ECL
Sept 20	Bolton Wanderers	Reebok Stadium	Drew 0–0	

Sept 24	Chelsea	Old Trafford	Drew 2–2	
Sept 27	Leeds United	Elland Road	Lost 0–1	
Oct 1	Juventus	Old Trafford	Won 3–2	ECL
Oct 4	Crystal Palace	Old Trafford	Won 2–0	
Oct 18	Derby County	Pride Park	Drew 2–2	
Oct 22	Feyenoord	Old Trafford	Won 2–1	ECL
Oct 25	Barnsley	Old Trafford	Won 7–0	
Nov 1	Sheffield Wed.	Old Trafford	Won 6–1	
Nov 5	Feyenoord	Rotterdam	Won 3–1	ECL
Nov 9	Arsenal	Highbury	Lost 2–3	
Nov 22	Wimbledon	Selhurst Park	Won 5–2	
Nov 27	FC Kosice	Old Trafford	Won 3–0	ECL
Nov 30	Blackburn Rovers	Old Trafford	Won 4–0	
Dec 5	Liverpool	Anfield	Won 3–1	
Dec 10	Juventus	Turin	Lost 0–1	ECL
Dec 15	Aston Villa	Old Trafford	Won 1–0	
Dec 21	Newcastle United	St James' Park	Won 1–0	
Jan 4	Chelsea	Stamford Bridge	Won 5–3	FA
Jan 10	Tottenham Hotspur	Old Trafford	Won 2–0	
Jan 19	Southampton	The Dell	Lost 0–1	
Jan 24	Walsall	Old Trafford	Won 5–0	FA
Jan 31	Leicester City	Old Trafford	Lost 0–1	
Feb 7	Bolton Wanderers	Old Trafford	Drew 1–1	
Feb 15	Barnsley	Old Trafford	Drew 1–1	FA
Feb 18	Aston Villa	Villa Park	Won 2–0	
Feb 21	Derby County	Old Trafford	Won 2–0	
Feb 25	Barnsley	Oakwell	Lost 2–3	FA
Feb 28	Chelsea	Stamford Bridge	Won 1–0	
Mar 4	AS Monaco	Monaco	Drew 0–0	ECL
Mar 11	West Ham United	Upton Park	Drew 1–1	
Mar 14	Arsenal	Old Trafford	Lost 0–1	
April 6	Blackburn Rovers	Ewood Park	Won 3–1	
April 10	Liverpool	Old Trafford	Drew 1–1	
April 18	Newcastle United	Old Trafford	Drew 1–1	
April 27	Crystal Palace	Selhurst Park	Won 3–0	

Key
CS = Charity Shield, ECL = European Champions' League, FA = FA Cup

Season 1998/99

FA CARLING PREMIERSHIP

	P	W	D	L	F	A	Pts
Manchester United	**38**	**22**	**13**	**3**	**80**	**37**	**79**
Arsenal	38	22	12	4	59	17	78
Chelsea	38	20	15	3	57	30	75
Leeds United	38	18	13	7	62	34	67
West Ham United	38	16	9	13	46	53	57
Aston Villa	38	15	10	13	51	46	55
Liverpool	38	15	9	14	68	49	54
Derby County	38	13	13	12	40	45	52
Middlesbrough	38	12	15	11	48	54	51
Leicester City	38	12	13	13	40	46	49
Tottenham Hotspur	38	11	14	13	47	50	47
Sheffield Wednesday	38	13	7	18	41	42	46
Newcastle United	38	11	13	14	48	54	46
Everton	38	11	10	17	42	47	43
Coventry City	38	11	9	18	39	51	42
Wimbledon	38	10	12	16	40	63	42
Southampton	38	11	8	19	37	64	41
Charlton Athletic	38	8	12	18	41	56	36
Blackburn Rovers	38	7	14	17	38	52	35
Nottingham Forest	38	7	9	22	35	69	30

EUROPEAN CHAMPIONS' LEAGUE GROUP D

	P	W	D	L	F	A	Pts
Bayern Munich	6	3	2	1	9	6	11
Manchester United	**6**	**2**	**4**	**0**	**20**	**11**	**10**
Barcelona	6	2	2	2	11	9	8
Brondby	6	1	0	5	4	18	3

Quarter-final: Manchester United beat Internazionale Milan 3–1 on aggregate
Semi-final: Manchester United beat Juventus 4–3 on aggregate
Final: Manchester United beat Bayern Munich 2–1

Schmeichel's appearances

(in League except where noted)

Date	Opponents	Venue	Score	
Aug 9	Arsenal	Wembley	Lost 0–3	CS
Aug 12	LKS Lodz	Old Trafford	Won 2–0	ECL
Aug 15	Leicester City	Old Trafford	Drew 2–2	
Aug 22	West Ham United	Upton Park	Drew 0–0	
Aug 26	LKS Lodz	Lodz	Drew 0–0	ECL
Sept 9	Charlton Athletic	Old Trafford	Won 4–1	
Sept 12	Coventry City	Old Trafford	Won 2–0	
Sept 16	Barcelona	Old Trafford	Drew 3–3	ECL
Sept 20	Arsenal	Highbury	Lost 0–3	

Sept 24	Liverpool	Old Trafford	Won 2–0	
Sept 30	Bayern Munich	Munich	Drew 2–2	ECL
Oct 21	Brondby	Copenhagen	Won 6–2	ECL
Oct 24	Derby County	Pride Park	Drew 1–1	
Oct 31	Everton	Goodison Park	Won 4–1	
Nov 4	Brondby	Old Trafford	Won 5–0	ECL
Nov 8	Newcastle United	Old Trafford	Drew 0–0	
Nov 14	Blackburn Rovers	Old Trafford	Won 3–2	
Nov 21	Sheffield Wed.	Hillsborough	Lost 1–3	
Nov 25	Barcelona	Barcelona	Drew 3–3	ECL
Nov 29	Leeds United	Old Trafford	Won 3–2	
Dec 5	Aston Villa	Villa Park	Drew 1–1	
Dec 9	Bayern Munich	Old Trafford	Drew 1–1	ECL
Dec 12	Tottenham Hotspur	White Hart Lane	Drew 2–2	
Dec 16	Chelsea	Old Trafford	Drew 1–1	
Dec 19	Middlesbrough	Old Trafford	Lost 2–3	
Dec 26	Notts Forest	Old Trafford	Won 3–0	
Dec 29	Chelsea	Stamford Bridge	Drew 0–0	
Jan 3	Middlesbrough	Old Trafford	Won 3–1	FA
Jan 16	Leicester City	Filbert Street	Won 6–2	
Jan 24	Liverpool	Old Trafford	Won 2–1	FA
Jan 31	Charlton Athletic	The Valley	Won 1–0	
Feb 3	Derby County	Old Trafford	Won 1–0	
Feb 6	Notts Forest	City Ground	Won 8–1	
Feb 14	Fulham	Old Trafford	Won 1–0	FA
Feb 17	Arsenal	Old Trafford	Drew 1–1	
Feb 20	Coventry City	Highfield Road	Won 1–0	
Feb 27	Southampton	Old Trafford	Won 2–1	
Mar 3	Internazionale Milan	Old Trafford	Won 2–0	ECL
Mar 7	Chelsea	Old Trafford	Drew 0–0	FA
Mar 10	Chelsea	Stamford Bridge	Won 2–0	FA
Mar 13	Newcastle United	St James' Park	Won 2–1	
Mar 17	Internazionale Milan	Milan	Drew 1–1	ECL
Mar 21	Everton	Old Trafford	Won 3–1	
April 3	Wimbledon	Selhurst Park	Drew 1–1	
April 7	Juventus	Old Trafford	Drew 1–1	ECL
April 11	Arsenal	Villa Park	Drew 0–0	FA
April 14	Arsenal	Villa Park	Won 2–1	FA
April 21	Juventus	Turin	Won 3–2	ECL
April 25	Leeds United	Elland Road	Drew 1–1	
May 1	Aston Villa	Old Trafford	Won 2–1	
May 5	Liverpool	Anfield	Drew 2–2	
May 9	Middlesbrough	The Riverside	Won 2–1	
May 12	Blackburn Rovers	Ewood Park	Drew 0–0	
May 16	Tottenham Hotspur	Old Trafford	Won 2–1	
May 22	Newcastle United	Wembley	Won 2–0	FAF
May 26	Bayern Munich	Barcelona	Won 2–1	ECLF

Key
CS = Charity Shield, ECL = European Champions' League, ECL = European
Champions' League final, FA = FA Cup, FAF = FA Cup final

Peter Schmeichel's international appearances for Denmark

No.	Date	Opponents	Score
1	20.05.87	Greece	5–0
2	10.06.87	Rumania	8–0
3	03.09.87	Rumania	2–1
4	28.10.87	Poland	2–0
5	18.11.87	West Germany	0–1
6	30.03.88	West Germany	1–1
7	20.04.88	Greece	4–0
8	10.05.88	Hungary	2–2
9	18.05.88	Poland	3–0
10	05.06.88	Belgium	3–1
11	14.06.88	West Germany	0–2
12	17.06.88	Italy	0–2
13	31.08.88	Sweden	2–1
14	28.09.88	Iceland	1–0
15	19.10.88	Greece	1–1
16	02.11.88	Bulgaria	1–1
17	08.02.89	Malta	2–0
18	10.02.89	Finland	0–0
19	12.02.89	Algeria	0–0
20	22.02.89	Italy	0–1
21	12.04.89	Canada	2–0
22	26.04.89	Bulgaria	2–0
23	17.05.89	Greece	7–1
24	07.06.89	England	1–1
25	23.08.89	Belgium	0–3
26	06.09.89	Holland	2–2
27	11.10.89	Rumania	3–0
28	15.11.89	Rumania	1–3
29	05.02.90	U.A.E.	1–1
30	14.02.90	Egypt	0–0
31	11.04.90	Turkey	1–0
32	15.05.90	England	0–1
33	30.05.90	West Germany	0–1
34	05.09.90	Sweden	1–0
35	11.09.90	Wales	1–0
36	10.10.90	Faroe Islands	4–1
37	17.10.90	Northern Ireland	1–1
38	14.11.90	Yugoslavia	0–2
39	01.05.91	Yugoslavia	2–1
40	05.06.91	Austria	2–1
41	12.06.91	Italy	0–2*
42	15.06.91	Sweden	0–4
43	25.09.91	Faroe Islands	4–0
44	09.10.91	Austria	3–0
45	13.11.91	Northern Ireland	1–1
46	29.04.92	Norway	1–0
47	03.05.92	Soviet Union	1–1
48	11.06.92	England	0–0
49	14.06.92	Sweden	0–1
50	17.06.92	France	2–1
51	22.06.92	Holland	2–2†
52	26.06.92	Germany	2–0
53	26.08.92	Latvia	0–0
54	09.09.92	Germany	1–2
55	23.09.92	Lithuania	0–0
56	14.10.92	Republic of Ireland	0–0
57	18.11.92	Northern Ireland	1–0
58	24.02.93	Argentina	1–1‡
59	31.03.93	Spain	1–0
60	14.04.93	Latvia	2–0

61	28.04.93	Republic of Ireland	1–1
62	02.06.93	Albania	4–0
63	25.08.93	Lithuania	4–0
64	08.09.93	Albania	1–0
65	13.10.93	Northern Ireland	1–0
66	17.11.93	Spain	0–1
67	09.03.94	England	0–1
68	26.05.94	Sweden	1–0
69	01.06.94	Norway	1–2
70	17.08.94	Finland	2–1
71	07.09.94	Macedonia	1–1
72	12.10.94	Belgium	3–1
73	16.11.94	Spain	0–3
74	29.03.95	Cyprus	1–1
75	26.04.95	Macedonia	1–0
76	31.05.95	Finland	1–0
77	07.06.95	Cyprus	4–0
78	16.08.95	Armenia	2–0
79	06.09.95	Belgium	3–1
80	11.10.95	Spain	1–1
81	15.11.95	Armenia	3–1
82	27.03.96	Germany	0–2
83	24.04.96	Scotland	2–0
84	02.06.96	Ghana	1–0
85	09.06.96	Portugal	1–1
86	16.06.96	Croatia	0–3
87	19.06.96	Turkey	3–0
88	14.08.96	Sweden	1–0
89	01.09.96	Slovenia	2–0
90	09.10.96	Greece	2–1
91	09.11.96	France	1–0
92	29.03.97	Croatia	1–1
93	30.04.97	Slovenia	4–0
94	08.06.97	Bosnia-Herzegovina	2–0
95	20.08.97	Bosnia-Herzegovina	0–3
96	10.09.97	Croatia	3–1
97	11.10.97	Greece	0–0
98	22.04.98	Norway	0–2
99	28.05.98	Sweden	0–3
100	05.06.98	Cameroon	1–2
101	12.06.98	Saudi Arabia	1–0
102	18.06.98	South Africa	1–1
103	24.06.98	France	1–2
104	28.06.98	Nigeria	4–1
105	03.07.98	Brazil	2–3
106	19.08.98	Czech Republic	0–1
107	05.09.98	Belarus	0–0
108	10.02.99	Croatia	1–0
109	27.03.99	Italy	1–2
110	28.04.99	South Africa	1–1
111	05.06.99	Belarus	1–0
112	09.06.99	Wales	2–0
113	18.08.99	Holland	0–0
114	04.09.99	Switzerland	2–1
115	08.09.99	Italy	3–2

*After extra time
†Denmark won 5–4 on penalties
‡Argentina won 5–4 on penalties

Overall record

P	W	L	D	F	A
115	59	28	28	168	96

Index